Let Your Solo Style Shine!

Developing your own signature style takes time. It means figuring out what trends and styles look best on you, and then being confident enough— with yourself and with what you wear—to get out there and strut your stuff!

Everyone has a style, which comes across in everything you do, from what you wear to your BFF's birthday bash to your sneaks-and-ponytail weekends. In *The Girls' Life Guide to Being a Style Superstar!*, you'll find everything you need to know from A to Z on:

- ✳ *what* to wear
- ✳ *how* to wear it
- ✳ *where* to find it and
- ✳ what to wear *with* it!

This book will (hopefully) inspire you to explore your inner fashion self. Whether you're into pseudo punk or funk, go for girly frills, or veer on the sporty side, clothes can express your unique personality. Think wearing jeans and tees all the time means you don't have a "look"? Wrong! You can turn that casual outfit into a classic fashion statement that screams "YOU!" just by adding a scarf, boots, or a blazer—this book will show you how. With tips on how to build a basic wardrobe, accessory suggestions and garment care, *GL* has your clothing qualms covered! And remember, you don't need expensive clothes to pull

off diva-licious looks. As long as you know what styles look best on YOU, you can be a fashion queen no matter what.

You'll also get how-tos for creating your own unique styles, ways to keep that closet under control, and smart shopping tips. But most of all, you'll get tips for being a healthy, confident you. So, read on! *GL's* style savvy advice will have you rockin' the best looks for school, fun, and forever!

Karen

Karen Bokram
Editor-in-Chief, *GL*

Chapter 1

Your Inner Fashionista: Discovering Your Personal Style

What you wear reveals a lot about you—and just about everyone (even that fuddy-duddy science teacher) has a look that says something about her personality. After all, clothes aren't just to keep us warm (or to help us beat the heat!)—they're one of the major ways we show the world who we are, what we like, and what we're all about.

But to make the most of your look— whatever it is!—first, you've got to determine your inner style sensibility. So, check out the quiz that follows to determine your personal sense of style, then read on for some stylish and fashionable tips on how to whip up the right outfit for any occasion—whether it's just dinner with the fam, hangin' at your best bud's slumber party, or—*gulp*—giving an oral presentation in front of your classmates!

Style Savvy: What's Your Style Sense?

Figuring out your personal style can be tricky, but this quiz will get you on your way to finding your inner fashionista. Answer the following questions and then tally up your score to find out your superstar style.

1. **It's the first day of school. You:**

   a. want to make a great first impression. You've had your clothes picked out for days: a simple black dress, vintage cardigan, and black leather flats.

   b. throw on your favorite old jeans, layer a couple of new tees, one with a vintage print on it, and wrap your waist in a black studded belt.

   c. wear a pink sundress, matching nail polish, and shoes that have a bit of a heel.

   d. think it's no big deal. It's just like any other day, right? You throw on your most comfy sweatpants, your favorite tee, and tennis sneaks —and you're out the door.

2. **It's winter holiday time at your grandma's and the whole family will be there. You:**

   a. wear something festive, but not too flashy. Probably black velvet.

   b. don a funky, bright-colored mod coat with black pants and this season's boots.

   c. show off your new cranberry-colored swirly dress, which you've paired with sparkly earrings and an up-do.

   d. swap the sweatpants for jeans and your fave hoody sweatshirt—this is a dressy event, after all!

3. **Your best friend just bought an outfit that everyone else is wearing. You:**

   a. think it looks great on her (and everyone else), but wearing the latest fad is not your scene.

   b. definitely like the look, but want to make it your own. You get the top in a different color than your pal's, and pair it with a vintage skirt and ankle boots.

   c. think the whole get-up looks way too boyish. Pass!

   d. don't even notice. Who's wearing what?

4. **There's a new boy at school who's a total hottie. How are you going to catch his eye?**

   a. By blowing him away with your brain power.

   b. He's sure to double-take you in your designer jeans, which even *you* have to admit look good on you.

   c. He won't be able to miss your glossy, shiny hair (that you brush 100 strokes before you go to bed) and your strawberry-glossed lips.

   d. Once he sees how skilled you are on your skateboard, you'll be riding the half-pipe together.

5. **Your best bud has invited you on a family vacation. You pack:**

   a. everything according to color: Black, white, navy, and beige.

   b. nearly everything in your closet; you never know what you might need.

   c. dresses, skirts, and tops—all in light, pastel colors and flowered prints.

   d. sweats, some jeans, and lots of athletic shoes—you're hoping to be outdoors the whole time, playing some kind of sport.

6. **You and your pals are going to the park for a jog. There's a high chance the neighborhood cuties will be there shooting hoops. How do you dress?**

   a. Vintage jogging pants complete with matching sneakers.

   b. Yoga pants and your fave band t-shirt.

   c. A matching velour sweat-suit in pink, light blue, or white.

   d. Sweat-shorts, a jog-tank, and running shoes.

7. **You've scored tickets to the hottest concert of the year. You:**

   a. go for a skirt and sweater in a totally neutral color scheme—you want to look nice, but low-key.

   b. dress up your 'do with color and sport black rubber bangles around your wrist.

   c. choose a circle skirt and flutter-sleeve blouse.

   d. slip on (at the last minute!) jeans, a sweater, and a pair of Converse All-Stars.

8. **You're trying out for the lead in the school play. You want to go for a dramatic look, so you wear a:**

a. black turtleneck and dark pants.

b. sailor-y white top with navy stripes and a pair of jeans. It's fun, but not too loud.

c. red dress. You want to get noticed!

d. baseball cap and sunglasses.

9. **It's the weekend and you're hanging out at home with the fam. How do you look?**

a. Casual in your weekend clothes: Capris and a simple white cotton tee.

b. Ready for action: Cargo pants and a printed t-shirt.

c. Like you're going to the mall: Hair done, lip gloss on.

d. You're lounging in your PJs. You're hanging out at home, for goodness sake! Who's going to see you?!?

10. **Your perfect gift to receive would be:**

a. something simple, but elegant, like a pair of earrings or a purse.

b. a subscription to your favorite fashion mag.

c. a gift certificate to a boutique in the mall.

d. tickets to a hockey game, or other sporting event.

11. **Your favorite accessory is:**

a. a simple piece of jewelry.

b. shoes, belts, bags—you like everything and enjoy mixing stuff together.

c. sparkly barrettes.

d. accessory? What's that?

SCORING ★ ★ ★ ★ ★ ★ ★

Mostly As: Classic.

Your style is timeless and glamorous. You have a knack for knowing what looks good on you and how to wear it. A peek in your closet reveals a color palette of neutrals (black, white, beige, tan, navy, and gray). To add some WOW to your wardrobe for special occasions, mix one or two trendy pieces in with your classics. Or get playful with accessories, like earrings, purses, and shoes.

Mostly Bs: Modern.

You like to dance to your own beat when it comes to style. You use fashion to express yourself and aren't afraid of mixing all kinds of styles together. To you, fashion is an adventure, worthy of taking clothing risks. However, you do need to make sure you don't go overboard. Since you gravitate toward wild colors and trends, make sure you have plenty of classic pieces in your wardrobe to round out your look and make your styles last longer. Also, keep in mind the event you're dressing for. When dressing for your grandmother's birthday, save the studs and your fave punk look for hanging with your pals.

Mostly Cs: Girly.

Whoa, Princess! You are super-feminine and love anything frilly, fuzzy, soft, or cuddly, and your closet is probably chock-full of pale pinks, blues, and pearls. It's likely you're never seen without your hair done or lip gloss on, and you probably prefer dresses or skirts over pants. While it's good to be in touch with your inner girly-girl, you don't always have to be so done-up. Loosening up will help you feel more comfortable in your natural skin. Also, if you add some pants to your wardrobe—paired with a flutter-sleeve top, you'll still look like your girly self.

Mostly Ds: Sporty.

You'd rather be skateboarding or playing basketball than figuring out what to wear. As long as you're comfortable, you don't really care what you wear. And it's definitely important to feel comfortable. But, you've got to get out of the sweatpants sometimes, girl! You just need to spice up your all-sweat wardrobe with some basic, casual pieces that are still comfy, but will make you look a whole lot more put-together. Cargo pants and khakis are good, sporty alternatives for you.

Fad vs. Style ★ ★ ★ ★ ★ ★ ★ ★ ★ ★ ★ ★

Before you get dressed, here's a quick lesson in Fashion 101. Think about your favorite celebrity. Chances are, you've seen pics of her sporting a trendy designer outfit you and your buds found positively over the top. Because she's often in the spotlight, it's her job to look hip, which means she's sometimes caught on camera sporting a get-up that's *way* out there.

Here's the thing: There's a big difference between fad and style. Fads and trends are usually created by a designer, splashed all over magazines, worn on TV and in movies, and long-gone once summer turns to fall. Style, on the other hand, can be as one-of-a-kind as personality, and it's timeless. Style is what oozes from a girl who knows how to wear her clothes, understands when to wear them, and feels fabulous in them. Really, style is all about having a well-stocked arsenal of self-confidence. If you feel good about yourself, you can look good in just about anything (okay, maybe not *anything*, but you get the idea!). Once you're equipped with great style secrets, you can use clothes to do a lot more than keep your bod covered. You can use shirts, skirts, tops, bottoms, shoes, and accessories to express yourself. Think of it this way: **You're a canvas and clothes are the paint!**

Keys to Looking Good and Feeling Great ★ ★ ★ ★

Think all ya gotta do is check the tag and pull the dress over your head? Well, not quite, stylie. What's just as important as making sure clothes are right for you is being sure they *fit* right on you! Even worse than rockin' the wrong look, the wrong fit can derail a potentially fabulous look. But don't worry—follow these tips to take your fit from fine to fabulous!

In the Dressing Room: Finding the Right Fit

You can probably relate to this scene: You're in the fitting room, trying on tons of back-to-school clothes, and nothing, absolutely NOTHING, fits right. But don't worry—you're not the only one who's experienced fitting-room frenzy. With all the different body types, sizes, and shapes in the world, it'd be weird if you could yank on those jeans with no problem the first time. The best way to avoid a makeover meltdown is to forget what's hot this season, and concentrate on what looks great on YOU—whether it's in or not. Because when you look fab, you're always in style. Read on for some tips on finding a fabulous fit:

👕 Clothes should skim your bod, floating neatly over your figure.

👕 Pass on stuff that's skin-tight. Not only are tight clothes uncomfortable, they also get super-creased and you won't look your best. Better to go for the next size up.

👕 Forget about baggy items. Clothes that are too big make you look bigger—or, super-small! If you want to look just right, find clothes that really fit.

- When choosing long-sleeved shirts, jackets, or coats, make sure the sleeves end just over your wrist bone. If sleeves are too short, the top will look too small on you. If the sleeves are too long, it will look too big.

- For the best length, the hem of your pants should almost touch the top of your shoes—that is, unless you're going for Capris or other pants that are supposed to be short. Those should fall about mid-calf.

- Remember that clothes marked "100% Cotton" will shrink in the wash. If the item feels at all snug, choose the next size up!

- Seams, pockets, and any other details should lie flat when you sit or stand—to give you a smooth line.

- Pleats are tricky—when you wear them, go for a skirt with pleats that begin below your hip line, not at the waist.

- Steer clear of shiny, clingy fabrics—they give everyone funny bumps and bulges.

- When choosing clothes with stripes, remember: Vertical stripes make your body look longer, while horizontal ones make you look wider. Don't mix stripes going different ways in one outfit!

- Wear pants that are comfortable and can be easily buttoned, zipped, or snapped. Don't wear pants that you have to lie down or suck in your stomach to get on! You'll go through the day with a big tummy-ache—for what?

- And, most important, don't buy clothes that don't fit you, thinking you'll grow into them some day. By the time they fit, it's likely they'll be outdated, or that you'll no longer like their style.

It's Just a Number: Finding the "Right" Size

Try this on for size: There is NO perfect size. (That's right: Nope. Nada. None.) As you grow, your body is going to change, and your size will change with it! Style has nothing to do with size—it's all about fit. So, don't get stressed over a tag! Besides, there is no standard size—designers, labels, cuts, and fabrics fit everyone's bod differently, so size doesn't mean much when figuring out what fits YOU best. Also, part of finding fabulous style is feeling totally comfortable in your own skin, no matter what size you are. So, push the tag back and focus on fit.

So, now that you see that individual size doesn't matter, it's important to know what your basic size is—this will save you from dressing-room drama in the future. To figure out what size you are, you should know your measurements (ask a pal or your Mom to help with this). You're gonna need some measuring tape—not the one that snaps back in the metal can, but the fabric tape you can wind all the way around your body. Here's how to measure yourself:

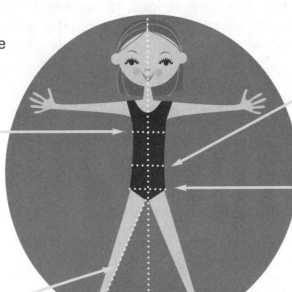

Chest:
Threading the tape around your arms and sides, measure around the fullest part of your chest.

Waist:
Measure around your natural waistline.

Hips:
Pulling the tape down from your waistline, find the widest part at the top of your legs, and measure.

Inseam:
Wearing a pair of pants, measure from the top inner pant leg seam to the bottom hem.

Height:
Measure from the tip-top of your head to your tootsies. Along your back, from head to heel works best.

Now that you've got your measurements in place, check out the following charts for a general size guideline:

GIRL SIZES

SIZE	AGE	HEIGHT	WAIST
M/7-8	7-8	49-55"	22.5-23.5"
L/9-10	9-10	55-57"	24-24.5"
XL/11-12	11-12	57-60"	25-25.5"
XXL/13-14	13-14	60-65"	25.5-27"

JUNIOR OR WOMEN'S SIZES

SIZE	CHEST	WAIST	HIP	INSEAM
XS/1-2	32"	24"	34"	27"
S/4	33"	25"	35"	28"
M/6	34"	26"	36"	29"
L/8	35"	27"	37"	29"
XL/10	36"	28"	38"	29"
XXL/12	37"	29"	39"	29"

It's a good idea to check your measurements every six months or so, because your size will likely change a bit over time. You also might want to jot your size down in a small notebook to have handy for trips to the mall. Plus, one brand's size 0 is another brand's size 2, so you need to try everything on and figure out which brands or labels fit you best.

Style Secret:

Most celebs have tailors, who hem, stitch, and re-sew their clothes so their outfits hang perfectly. But guess what? Usually for a modest fee, a store—or your local dry-cleaner!—will hem or let out your pants, take in wide waists, or otherwise dart and fit your duds to perfection. So, don't be shy—ask about the service, or have your Mom give your own clothes a going-over with a needle and thread.

Yay or No Way? ★ ★ ★ ★ ★ ★ ★ ★ ★ ★ ★ ★ ★ ★ ★

Have you ever worn something that seemed like a great idea when you were pulling it out of the closet, but by the time you got to school, you realized it was a fashion no-no? Or maybe you borrowed your big sis's fave new outfit, which looked fab on her, but bad on you? Knowing what to wear and what to avoid for your body type will help you keep your style sense in tip-top shape. Keep these things in mind when choosing what to wear:

If you're petite:

Just because you're not long in the leg department doesn't mean you can't have smashin' style. You just have to be aware of what's a really great look for your shape.

* Try wearing the same color, or the same shade, from your noggin to your clogs. A monochromatic color scheme (single color) will make you look long and lean.

* Short skirts in solid colors will also be flattering; they will make your legs look longer.

* If you don't want to shrink an inch or too, avoid jeans that are waaay flared or super wide-legged—the wider they are, the shorter you'll look!

* Put the kibosh on too many bows, ribbons, or ruffles—if you don't want to look younger than you are.

* Need a dress for your BFF's birthday party? Go for slim silhouettes, like a straight dress that skims your body, a wrap dress, or a shirtdress.

* Be sure to keep dresses pretty simple—the smaller you are, the more overwhelming details can be on the outfit overall.

✳ Shirts with high waists will make your legs look longer, while skirts with low waists can actually take off an inch or two of your height.

✳ Cropped pants take an inch or two off your length, so go for thick-soled slides to add height, or stick with long, slim, dark-colored pants or jeans.

If you're tall:

If you're tall, you can probably fit into junior sizes, which means you have a ton of style options. Just remember these simple rules for tall frames:

✳ Skirts and tops will keep you looking balanced and proportioned, while straight dresses can make you look like one long line—go for shapely dresses to give movement to your outfits, or break up the long line by throwing a cardigan sweater or fun jacket over your shoulders.

✳ Try jeans with a flare-leg fit; they'll highlight your long legs. Straight-leg jeans will also be flattering, if you're looking for more of a classic look.

✳ Simple lines look best on your frame; pass on lots of details or frilly accents.

✳ V-necks will elongate your neckline, and make you look elegant and glamorous.

✳ An empire—high—or a dropped-waist dress can be an awesome option for tall gals.

✳ Cropped pants, boyish jeans, and men's-style trousers look fabulous on your leggy frame.

If you're thin:

Slight girls can look smashing in a variety of get-ups—here are some options if you're stylin' and slim:

* Layers work great and can add a pound or two to your look. Pair a thin tee or tank under a thicker tee, or try long sleeves under short in fall and winter.

* Funky patterns or prints can add zing to your step, and they'll make your style seem larger than life.

* Horizontal-striped shirts or pants work great on you; they add breadth to your top and fill you out.

* Sweaters in bulky fabrics, like wool, can add pounds to your slim shape.

* You can layer a tee or tank under a sweater for more padding.

* Go for jeans that are straight leg, or, if you're flarin', make sure you've got a nice, smooth fit—they shouldn't be baggy.

* If it's party time, try dresses that go in at the waist, like shirt and wrap dresses, or accessorize by adding a cool belt to your dressy outfit. It will call attention to your slim waist.

* Go for bias-cut skirts—this angled cut makes the fabric cling, which is perfect for your figure, and will add some shape.

* Look for shrunken versions of boy shirts. Sometimes, you can find the coolest printed tees this way.

* Oversize sweaters can overwhelm your slim frame—a chunky sweater will give you the same look without leaving you flappin' fabric in the breeze.

If you're plus-sized:

For large-sized knockout style, find the looks that fit your shape best, and you'll be wearing winning duds forever.

* Use patterns to add accents—try a great scarf or a bright cardigan with dark or muted jeans.

* Long or three-quarter sleeves can add length and style to shapely arms.

* Keep styles simple. One choice detail is better for your shape than a lot of frills and ruffles.

* Skip the minis and go for longer, A-line skirts, which will lengthen and slim your lines.

* Go for vertical stripes to elongate, rather than horizontal stripes, which tend to widen.

* Stay away from ribbed fabrics, which add bulk. Go for smooth-textured fabrics, like cotton.

* When choosing jeans, avoid anything that's too tight. Also, stay away from back pockets that are spaced widely apart—they can add width in the back.

* Try flat-front skirt styles with side or back zippers. Pass on skirts with front darts—the two sewn lines across the tummy that pull a straight skirt in—and wrap skirts, which can bulge and pull.

* Don't try to camouflage with loose-fitting dresses. Loose dresses can look boxy and messy.

* Go for pants and jeans that are fitted through the hips and bottom and slightly wide-legged at the bottom to balance and highlight your frame.

Fabrics ★ ★ ★ ★ ★ ★ ★ ★ ★ ★ ★ ★ ★ ★ ★ ★

To really understand style, you've gotta know a bit about fabric. Fabric is the material your clothes are made with. It comes in a bunch of different textures, colors, and patterns, and is an important factor to consider when you're trying to get the best fit. If a fabric is too stiff, it can make you look bulky or boxy. If the fabric is shiny, it can spotlight different parts of the outfit—which can be good or bad, depending on what look you want.

There are two types of fabric: Knitted and woven. Knits, like cotton tees, silk socks, or nubbly wool sweaters, are usually softer, stretchable items. Woven fabrics, which feel harder and tighter, like denim or cotton twill, are really strong and should last a long time.

Quality of a fabric is really important. For your day-to-day clothing, natural, higher-quality fabrics such as wool or cotton will last longer, wear better, and feel better on your skin. Synthetic or man-made fabrics such as polyester, rayon, and nylon can discolor, retain odors, and be harder to clean. For your basic skirts, sweaters, blouses, and pants, you want to go for items made out of natural, quality fabrics, even though sometimes that means shelling out more cash. (Fabric content is always listed on the label of an item, so you can check it out.)

Don't knock out synthetics altogether, though. Sports and activewear are filled with so-called "smart" fabrics that wick (absorb sweat away from your body), keep out cold and wind, and—most important—keep you dry in a major downpour much better than ordinary old cotton. So, while a polyester blouse can't hold a candle to a silk one in terms of overall quality, a synthetic jacket or parka is where it's at on the slopes, and wind-blocking jogging pants have it over sloppy ol' sweats on a blustery day. (Be a smart shopper, however—though synthetics are cheaper, in general, a high-quality nylon parka can run you just as much as that fancy silk blouse!)

For your long-lasting, finer garments, look for the following on the labels:

* ✳ Wool crepe, wool gabardine, wool-microfiber blends
* ✳ Cotton
* ✳ Cotton blended with silk
* ✳ Flat knits
* ✳ Two-ply silks

For your sporty, outdoor clothing needs, check the labels for these:

* ✳ Fleece or micro-fleece
* ✳ Polyester fiber or microfiber
* ✳ Wicking or dri-fit
* ✳ Wind-repellent
* ✳ Water-repellent

Color Me Beautiful ★ ★ ★ ★ ★ ★ ★ ★ ★ ★ ★ ★

People say redheads can't wear purple, but what clothing colors look great on a gal isn't really determined by the color of her hair, but by the numerous shades underneath her skin that create the main color of her face. Your skin color is actually millions of different colors, but most people have a definite tinge that falls into one of the primary colors of blue, yellow, or red (some folks have a mix of these shades, meaning an orange, green, or violet tinge to them instead). When you dress to complement this shade, colors look great on you—and that's usually the reason someone says "Wow!" to how you look in your favorite sweater or dress.

To determine the primary color that's most dominant in your skin, take three pieces of colored paper that fall as close to the three primaries—red, blue, and yellow—as possible. Hold each up to your face, one after the other. Which one seems to meld in? Which one definitely clashes? If red looks just peachy, you're a ruddy girl. Does yellow seem to match? Hey, guess what—you've got some yellow in you, girl! (Hint: Determining colors is even more fun with a BFF—she can tell if you're kinda blue...while you can let her know she's positively green with envy!)

After you've figured out your color, read on for the best colors for each undertone...and for smashin' seasonal advice, too! (Hint—if you fall in between one of the primary colors, you're twice as nice! Play mix 'n' match with the shades from both.)

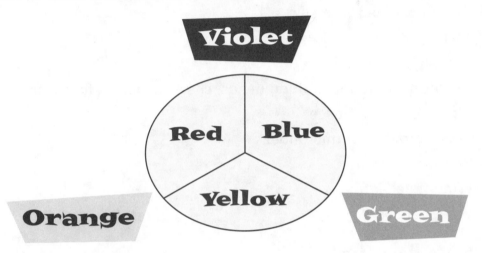

Red Undertones

Your strong, ruddy coloring can sometimes overpower the color of your clothing. That's why you should stick with a soft palette of pastels that complement and bring out your healthy, hearty skin tones.

Winter: Off-white, navy/black, strong brown

Spring: Pale pinks, soft yellow, baby blues

Summer: French blue, sea green, ivory

Fall: Pale orange, soft khaki, buff

Blue Undertones

Blue undertones give you a bold, classic look, and mean you can handle deep, strong colors! Don't shy away in florals—blue gals can be bold!

Winter: Bright white, chocolate, crimson red

Spring: Deep pink, seaglass green, turquoise blue

Summer: Bright orange, lemon yellow, ruby red

Fall: Wine, pine green, navy blue

Yellow Undertones

Girls with yellow undertones have a warm, earthy vibe and can wear distinct, bright colors like nobody else. Dig in!

Winter: Olive green, oak brown, eggplant

Spring: Blue-y green, curry yellow, warm fuschia

Summer: Ivory, golden brown, flame orange

Fall: Burnt orange, rust, camel

Patterns ★ ★ ★ ★ ★ ★ ★ ★ ★ ★ ★ ★ ★ ★ ★ ★

Okay, so now you know what fabric is made out of and what your colors are, but clothes also come in lots of different *patterns*. Here are some quick pattern facts—some of this you probably already know:

 **Prints:** fabrics with pictures or designs

 **Stripes:** fabric with vertical lines

 **Checks:** squares of color

 **Stripes:** fabric with horizontal lines

 **Polka-dots:** circles, large or small

 **Plaid:** intersecting lines

* When wearing patterns, you should usually team a solid bottom with a patterned top, or vice versa.

* Want to go for prints, but keep your classic style? Checks, pinstripes, and plaids are more classic, less trendy.

* Go ahead and experiment mixing patterns with each other, but when you do, make sure the colors are the same shade, and that one print is bigger than the other. For example, a green paisley blouse and blue striped pants are a no-no, but pair those same blue striped pants with a blue-polka-dotted blouse in the same shades— or a sailor top with the same-shade stripes running horizontally!

Style Secret: De-coding European Size Charts

As if it wasn't difficult enough to decipher American sizes, many stores carry European-sized clothes, which are measured in centimeters instead of inches. Don't worry, we've got you covered. Use the following charts to decode European sizes.

GIRLS

USA	European (cm)	UK (inches)
8	150	55
10	155	58
12	160	60

JUNIORS/WOMEN'S

USA	European (cm)	UK (inches)
4	34	6
6	36	8
8	38	10
10	40	12
12	42	14
14	44	16
16	46	18
18	48	20
20	50	22

Style Q & A

Q: I'm really sporty, but lately I've wanted to work a few more girly pieces into my wardrobe. How can I get a little more feminine without freaking myself out by pink stuff and lace?

A: It's easy to up your girly factor without looking like you've gone frills-crazy—the key is making small, but key, changes. Say you usually wear cargos and a T-shirt in the spring. Try switching your plain pants to a knee-length cargo skirt for a sporty, but sleek look. Or, keep the cargos, but switch that old tee to a peasant blouse with puff sleeves. Same goes for shoes—slowly work in sporty, but feminine, styles like leather Mary Janes, riding boots, and/or slim slides to alternate with your normal sneaks routine. Soon enough, if you decide to work up to lace in your outfits, you won't even bat an eye!

Q: I have three older sisters, so I always receive a lot of hand-me-downs. How can I get an individual look when I'm stuck wearing someone else's clothes?

A: You're in a tough position. True, you get a way bigger wardrobe than lots of girls, but you don't get to choose the clothes that are in it! What's more, some of your duds may be worn, ill-fitting, or out of style by the time you get them. How to cope? You've heard this before, but now's the time to really put those creative juices to work. You might think you're stuck wearing yesterday's clothes, but you've really got a wealth of fashion options that can yield you a wardrobe any girl would envy, if you concentrate on the following: a) Fixing up old duds to look new, b) thinking of new ways to wear them, and c) mixing in a few basics.

Look at it this way: You might have what were your sis's favorite jeans, but with a little sewing help from Mom, they can become a cool skirt or cut-off shorts for you. And though you think you've inherited a dorky blazer, with a few rhinestones added, it can be a glam match for another sis's old linen skirt—which, by the way, you've shortened a few inches, and now wear with a baby tee in the spring instead. Best of all? You've finally got the suede jacket another sis saved up to buy five years ago—and since it's been so long, it's back in style!

Q: I tried to do the color thing, but nothing looks right on me. Does this mean no colors look good on me?

A: Of course not! Sometimes, people have such an interesting mix of colors in their faces that finding one "right" color scheme is hard. So, here's what you do: Grab a BFF, and lay out all your favorite clothes. Then, one after another, hold the garments up to your face. Which ones look awesome? Ho-hum? Positively…awful? Lay out the ones you agree make you look great, and make a note of these colors for the future. (Hint: Try to find a yellowish tone, a red tone, and a blue tone that look good on you so you have the most options.) Then, the next time you go shopping…head straight for those shades! You'll be colorin' crazy in no time.

5 RULES FOR THE ROAD

Don't wear things that:

1. Don't fit properly

2. Don't suit you, just because they're stylish

3. Make you fumble and fidget

4. Are so difficult to clean, you'll never wear them

5. Clash!

Chapter 2

In Your Closet

How many times have you stood in front of your closet and moaned, "I've got nothing to wear!"? For most of us, that scene probably happens every morning! But chances are, you've got plenty to wear—maybe even too much! (T-shirt heaps, anyone?) What you need is a little guidance on how and when to wear your duds—and ways to organize your closet that will have you stylin' and smilin' out the door in a flash. Keep reading, and you'll never scratch your head again about what to slip into.

Pulling It Together ★ ★ ★ ★ ★ ★ ★ ★ ★ ★

Great style starts with having a wardrobe that's full of timeless basics you can mix and match with trendy accessories or bright colors. Every girl's closet should include a great-fitting pair of jeans, some pants other than jeans, comfy tees (long- and short-sleeved), tops, sweaters, dresses, skirts, a jacket, and a good winter coat. But there are so many different cuts and styles—how do you keep them all straight? Do you know the difference between boot-cut and flare-leg jeans...or what a cap sleeve is? Read on...we'll de-stress the dress and get you in the know with your clothes!

Jeans ★

Jeans are a staple of just about everyone's wardrobe. The right pair can be as comfy and soothing as your old baby blanket. But there are so many brands and cuts, how do you find the pair that's right for you?

First, you need to brush up on common jean styles:

Flare leg: Jeans are fitted at the top and flare at the bottom.

Boot cut: Jeans are fitted at the top and throughout the leg, flared just a bit to fit over boots.

Wide leg: Jeans are fitted at the top with wide legs starting from the hip.

Boy cut: Jeans are cut more square through the hip, with a straighter leg.

Straight leg: Jeans are fitted at the top and have straight legs, with no flare.

Capri: Jeans are shorter, hitting above the ankle, often mid-calf.

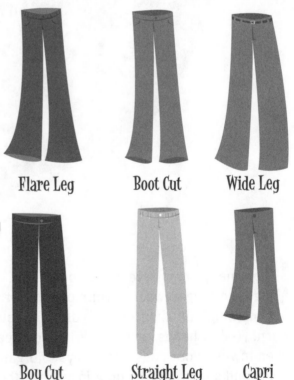

Flare Leg   Boot Cut   Wide Leg

Boy Cut   Straight Leg   Capri

Wear It

Now that you're in-the-know about cuts, you'll want to know what to look for when shopping for that perfect pair:

✳ The longer the jean leg, the taller you'll look. Just make sure the legs aren't so long that they hang way past the bottom of your shoes—you'll trip!

✳ If you're having trouble deciding on which color or shade of jeans to pick, dark-wash jeans are the most flattering to all shapes.

✳ Jeans that are baggy can add bulk.

✳ Larger, centered pockets on the backs of jeans make a clean, classic look.

✳ When wearing low-waisted jeans, add a belt to keep 'em up over your hip bones!

✳ When trying on jeans, be sure to sit down in them to make sure they're not too tight anywhere. Also, you should be able to stick your hands in the pockets. If you can't, they're too tight.

IN YOUR CLOSET

A good mix: One pair of dressy jeans, one pair of kick-arounds, and one pair of in-between jeans that could be dressed up or down. For some jammin' jean-looks, sprinkle in a pair of cords or white jeans.

Pants (Other Than Jeans) ★ ★ ★ ★ ★ ★ ★ ★ ★ ★

Even though it's tempting to wear jeans all the time (especially once you find your fave pair!), you'll want to wear other kinds of pants once in a while. Pants can be worn either dressy or casual, and there are plenty of styles that can stand in for your old blue jeans in terms of comfort, and spruce up your all-denim, all-the-time look.

Cargo: Cargo pants have pockets on the side legs—often many pockets—and have become almost as standard as jeans.

Wide leg: Like jeans, wide leg pants are fitted at the top and have wide legs, starting at the hips.

Sailor: Sailor pants are fitted at the top, usually with a flat, buttoned front, and have slightly wide legs, beginning at the hips. Sailor pants get their name from, well, sailors, who wear them.

Capri: Capris are shorter in length than other pants, tapered above the ankle.

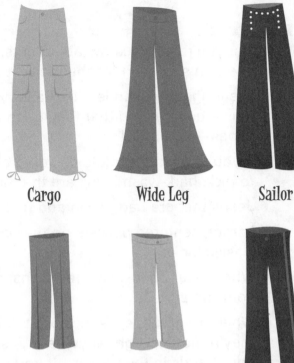

Cargo　　　Wide Leg　　　Sailor

Capri　　　Cropped

Dressy

Cropped: Cropped pants are shorter in length, like Capris, but aren't tapered.

Dressy: Dressy pants are fitted, often dark in color, and can come in festive fabrics like velvet or satin.

Wear It

Keep the following tips in mind when searching for pants:

* ✳ Pants with a little stretch in the fabric can offer a better fit.

* ✳ If you live in a cold climate, winter pants should be wool or a wool-blend (wool combined with a synthetic fabric such as polyester or acrylic).

* ✳ Summer pants should be a cool, breathable cotton or cotton-blend in a pastel or light shade. Light-colored fabrics, in addition to helping you look cool, actually bounce the heat off you, while dark-colored fabrics, which absorb sunlight, make you hotter.

IN YOUR CLOSET

A good mix: Two pairs of winter school pants (maybe a pair of wool wide legs and a pair of sailors), two pairs of spring school pants (which could include cargos and Capris), and one pair of dressy pants.

T-shirts ★ ★ ★ ★ ★ ★ ★ ★ ★ ★ ★ ★ ★ ★ ★

Like jeans, T-shirts seem to be part of our standard uniform. And why not? They're comfy, and they can be dressed up or down. Did you know tees come in a ton of styles? Read on!

Boat neck: Boat necks have wide, rounded collars and are slightly off-the-shoulder.

Scoop neck: Scoop necks have deep, rounded collars.

Polo: Polos have a suit-shirt collar look, but because the fabric is a floppy, T-shirt knit—not the stiff, hard weave that makes your fancy blouse collars stand up—these collars look casual.

Crew neck: Crew necks have rounded collars just below the neck.

V-neck: V-necks are exactly what they sound like—the collar is shaped like a V.

Tank: Tank tops are scoop-necked with no sleeves, and have large, scooped armholes.

Boat Neck   Scoop Neck

Polo   Crew Neck

V-neck   Tank

Shell: Shells, which you typically wear under a matching cardigan, are sleeveless tops. These puppies, which look just like a sweater with its arms cut off, also come in wool and cashmere.

Short-sleeved: Sleeves end in the middle of your upper arm.

Three-quarter sleeved: Sleeves end below your elbow but above your wrist.

Long-sleeved: Sleeves end at your wrist.

Cap-sleeved: Cap sleeves are like mini-short sleeves—they're a slight sleeve that curves out just over the shoulder, ending at your upper arm.

Shell   Short-sleeved

Three-quarter sleeved   Long-sleeved

Cap-sleeved

Style Secret: Tees Tease

Make a style statement by layering your tees. Keep the bottom layer thinner than the top, and stay in the same color range for both shirts.

Wear It

When looking for the right fit, here are a couple of T-shirt tricks.

✳ Go for tees in fabrics that aren't too thick. Thick fabrics add bulk and can be hot and sweaty in the warmer months—which is when you mostly wear tees!

✳ Avoid super-tight tees—they can mess up the line of your outfit. Tight tees are fine, but they shouldn't *stre-e-tch* when you've got them on. If they pull across your stomach and chest, ride up on your belly, or pull at stress-points in your arms, giving them a bulgy look, then they're too tight—go for a larger size.

IN YOUR CLOSET

A good mix: Two white T-shirts, two black or dark colored tees, four tank tops, and, for a dash of fun, a striped tee, maybe a polo, and a few solids in lively colors, with interesting details.

Tops (That Ain't Tees) ★ ★ ★ ★ ★ ★ ★ ★ ★ ★

Tops can become as indispensable as tees once you get used to wearing 'em. But what are the best ones for your style, and what do you wear them with? Let's get on *top* of the most terrific toppers!

Button-up: This shirt buttons up the front, with a pointy, suit-shirt collar. For men, these dress shirts are sometimes called "Oxfords".

Blouse: Blouses have a feminine cut and are usually made with a soft, light fabric.

Wrap: Wrap shirts wrap around the top, usually tying at the waist.

Flutter sleeve: Flutter sleeves have ruffled sleeves of any length.

Tunic: A tunic has long sleeves and usually ends at the hips.

Halter: Halter tops have front straps that fasten or tie around the back of your neck, like the strings of a bathing suit. They're great for really hot days, since they leave your upper back open.

Button-up

Blouse

Wrap

Flutter Sleeve

Tunic

Halter

Wear It

Blouses come in so many styles and shapes. Here are some things to keep in mind:

* Try to match your blouse's style to your skirt or pants. Got a flowy, lacy blouse? Pair it with a delicate skirt. Got a button-up? Pair it with crisp pants or some cool vintage jeans.

* Tighter tops look good worn with looser bottoms. That means your slim-fitting halter top is perfect for your flowy peasant skirt.

* An untucked blouse looks great as long as it hangs right above the hip bone. Shorter, it looks like your blouse is too small or like you've paired it with the wrong item, while much longer tops make you look like you're wearing a nightshirt.

* A wrap blouse, which pulls in tight at the waist, looks great with high-waisted, wide-legged pants, or with a skirt that flares out at the bottom. Think hourglass!

* Don't pair a flutter-sleeved blouse with your fluttery-bottomed skirt—the fluttery-ness will be overwhelming. Instead, contrast it with a denim skirt or a simple cotton skirt in a similar fabric.

IN YOUR CLOSET

*A good mix: Two casual tops (like blouses)
and two tops for dressy events that can be
worn with dressy pants or a skirt
(like a wrap shirt and a flutter sleeve).*

Sweaters ★ ★ ★ ★ ★ ★ ★ ★ ★ ★ ★ ★ ★ ★ ★ ★ ★

Sweaters can do a lot more than keep you warm. The 1950s were famous for "sweater girls," who wore their cashmere-buttoned cardigans backwards and started a style revolution. Nowadays, sweaters come in tons more styles and are terrific for chill days or for punching up a skirt and shirt. So, don't sweat it—just read on to get it!

Cardigan: Cardigans button up the front and can be either crew or V-neck.

Shell: A sleeveless top in the same fabric worn under your cardie.

V-neck: Sweaters with a V-shaped neckline.

Crew neck: Crew necks have a rounded collar, just below the neck.

Zipper: Zipper sweaters zip up the front. They often have hoods.

Turtleneck: Turtlenecks have high collars that cover your neck.

Cardigan

Shell

V-neck

Crew Neck

Zipper

Turtleneck

Fabric is another important factor when sweater searching. The best—and most expensive—sweater fabrics are wool, lambswool, cashmere, and angora. Wool is from sheep's fur, lambswool from a lamb's fur, cashmere from the hair of the Indian and Tibetan Kashmir goat, and angora from the hair of the Angora goat. (Don't worry—they only trim the hair, not the actual sheep, lambs, or goats!) But sweaters also come in cotton and man-made acrylic blends, which offer less expensive—though less long-lasting—options.

Style Secret:

You can layer sweaters that are too short to wear separately (after they've shrunken in the wash!) over tees.

Wear It

When looking for fit, follow the same rules you would for a T-shirt. Keep in mind the following sweater savvy advice:

* ✷ Sweaters should follow the natural line of your shape without being too tight.
* ✷ Stay away from sweaters that are too baggy. Otherwise, you end up looking like a bulky UPS package!
* ✷ Don't get wooed by this season's trendiest colors. If you're investing in a well-made sweater, like cashmere, go for neutral colors. That way, your sweater should last several seasons.

★ IN YOUR CLOSET

A good mix: Two fitted pullovers (these, unlike the button-ups, go over your head), two cardigans, one turtleneck, and a couple of always-handy zip-up sweaters.

Dresses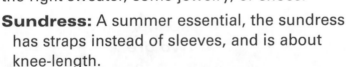

Dresses can be kind of tricky, because it can be tough finding a fit that works well on your whole bod. But once you find the right fit, a dress can become a staple of your look. You can use the same dress to go from casual to dressy, simply by adding the right sweater, some jewelry, or shoes.

Sundress

Strapless

Sundress: A summer essential, the sundress has straps instead of sleeves, and is about knee-length.

Strapless: Strapless dresses have no straps. Skirts are usually full, A-line (see the next section for description), or fitted.

Halter: Halters are sleeveless and fasten around the neck. They can have a fitted or full skirt.

Halter

Shift: Very basic, straight-cut dress with no real shape.

Long-sleeved: Long-sleeved dresses come in lots of styles and are great for the chillier months (duh!), or for elegant nighttime events, like concerts, where you may need to dress a bit warmer.

Shift   Long-sleeved

Wear It

Be prepared with this dress data:

* Strapless A-line dresses look good on just about every shape and size. If you get goosebumps, wrap a shawl around your shoulders.

* Need a dress for a dressy occasion? For fall and winter, you can't go wrong with black velvet. It's usually comfortable, and looks festive and dressy. For spring and summer? Any light-colored, linen dress is a cool, elegant showstopper—look for a synthetic linen blend to cut down on wrinkling.

* If you're wearing a simple dress, accessorize with jewelry, scarves, and hair clips. Or keep the accessories simple and go for a bold and bright dress.

* Be sure to sit down in the dress when you try it on. You don't want any surprise discomfort, or ill fit.

IN YOUR CLOSET

A good mix: Two sundresses for spring/summer, one cold-weather school dress, and two dressy dresses for more formal occasions (one for a formal event in the spring/summer, and one for winter/fall events).

Skirts ★ ★ ★ ★ ★ ★ ★ ★ ★

It's easy to get so used to wearing jeans and pants, and to forget that there's another option in the style toolbox: skirts. Skirts can be worn with everything from T-shirts to blouses.

A-line

Pleated

A-line: A-line skirts are fitted at the waist and bell out over the hips, making an A shape.

Pleated: Pleated skirts have folds in the fabric (pleats). School uniforms often include pleated skirts.

Pencil

Asymmetrical

Pencil: Pencil skirts hug the body and are narrow at the knees.

Asymmetrical: Asymmetrical skirts have a diagonal hemline.

Circle: Circle skirts are similar to A-lines, but have a fuller, rounder cut.

Mini: Mini-skirts can be in any of the above shapes or styles, but they fall above your knees! Avoid minis in the winter—duh!

Circle

Mini

Wear It

Don't skirt these issues!

* A-lines look great on just about everyone—they give every shape a slammin' line and keep you lookin' cool and elegant.

* Long skirts can make you look taller—and more formal! Wearing long skirts can be tricky, though, because you don't want your shape to get lost in all that fabric. If you wear long skirts, make sure they're fitted in the hips and hang almost to the floor.

* A skirt that hits the widest part of your calf can make your legs look all weird. Have it hemmed so it hits mid-knee.

✳ When wearing a mini, pair it with a top that doesn't reveal too much skin. Stay away from cropped tank tops paired with minis, unless it's a beach or pool party, where it's appropriate to show a little more skin.

✳ When trying on a skirt, move around in it. Make sure you can walk and swing comfortably.

IN YOUR CLOSET

A good mix: One denim skirt, two warm school skirts, two light summer skirts, and a dressy skirt. Each body looks good in different length and style skirts, so try a few on and ask your BFF or mom which suits you best. Are you an above-the-knee? A circle skirt? An A-line kind of gal? (Look great in all of them? Lucky you—you're versatile!) Once you've determined your best-fitting style, you can experiment with fabrics, lengths, and colors for even more looks.

Jackets ★ ★ ★ ★ ★ ★ ★ ★ ★ ★ ★ ★ ★ ★ ★ ★

Have you ever thought about adding jackets or blazers to your wardrobe? It may seem too stuffy or business-like, but not all jackets have to be like that. A blazer can be a fab way to dress up jeans, a skirt, or even a dress. And it might give you a star style none of your pals are sporting—making you unique!

Denim (or jean jackets): Denim jackets button up the front, have breast pockets, and visible stitching.

Military: A military jacket has a collar with lapels (those folded-back flaps on the front of Dad's jacket) and many buttons and pockets. It hits at your hips.

Denim

Military

Bomber: Bomber jackets are worn by Air Force pilots. They zip up the front, have a fitted band around the bottom, and a rounded collar. Originally, they were made out of leather to keep pilots warm and cut out the wind, but now, you can find them in all kinds of fabrics, including cotton, polyester, and nylon.

Bomber

Blazer

Blazer: Blazers are usually worn with suits. They have medium lapels, three buttons, and (often) front patch pockets.

Safari: Safari jackets, usually khaki or buff-colored in heavy cotton twill, are similar to denim jackets, but have more pockets and a boxier cut.

Safari

Wear It

Become a jacket junkie:

* You'd be surprised at how often you lift your arms in the real world. So, lift them in the dressing room! If your jacket's too tight in the arms and across the back, you can split a jacket just by leanin' over to pick up your book bag!

* Don't forget small details. Is it poochin' out in the back? Do the sleeves show too much wrist bone when you stretch? You may love the fabric, but if this fit isn't right for you, try to find something similar in a different style.

* Look for a lining! Linings—the fabric on the inside of your jacket—help a jacket fit smoothly, last longer, and keep you warmer. Go for lined jackets whenever possible.

* Getting bored with your old jacket fave? Don't buy a whole new one…just bust out some new buttons! Switching buttons is an inexpensive way to make a big difference. You can buy new buttons at any fabric store. With your mom's help, either take off the old ones and refasten the new, or have your dry-cleaner switch them.

Coats ★ ★ ★ ★ ★ ★ ★ ★ ★ ★ ★ ★ ★ ★ ★ ★ ★ ★

And you probably thought coats just kept you from getting frostbite. Wrong! They're a great way to let your personal style shine— especially when it's 10 degrees below zero—and it's the perfect topper to perfect your personal look.

Peacoat: Inspired by the Navy, a peacoat is usually navy blue or black wool, with a military-style collar and lots of buttons. These coats are double-breasted— that means you've got two lines of buttons, not just one, going down the front—and the coat ends at the hips.

Peacoat

Trench

Trench: Trench coats are longer (most often ending at the knee or a little below), button up the front, are belted around the waist, and are made of a water-resistant material usually in khaki, black, or beige. Many raincoats are made in the trench-coat style.

Belted overcoat: Similar to the trench, but the fabric is usually warmer and not water-resistant. They come in all lengths, from just below the waist to down to the tips of your toes.

Belted overcoat

Puffer

Puffer: Ski or snow jacket puffers are usually made of nylon. They have a layer of padding that makes them puffy, which can be down or a poly-blend, and sometimes a fleece shell. They can cinch in at the waist or go as long as knee-length, and sometimes they have detachable hoods.

Parka: Longer version of the puffer.

Windbreaker: A thin nylon jacket that zips up the front, and is good for windy spring weather.

Shearling: Shearlings are long, suede coats with sheepskin details.

Parka

Windbreaker

Shearling

Wear It

Wrap yourself up in full-length coat couture coverage:

* When trying on a coat, be sure to try it on over thick clothing, like sweaters. If you're only wearing a T-shirt, you could buy a size that's too small for the cold days when you're layered up.

* Coats should be comfortable and not feel tight anywhere. Lift up your arms and make sure there's no pulling in the armpits or shoulders.

* Be sure you can button a coat all the way up. It might look great open, but it won't feel great walking home in a snowstorm!

* Make sure your coat doesn't puff or gather anywhere—a coat should hang smoothly. If nothing in a particular style seems to fit right, try a different cut.

Whip Your Closet Into Shape: Organizing Your Clothes By Color

If rummaging through piles of disorganized clothes makes your getting-ready-in-the-morning time a total pain, then re-organizing your closet may be just what you need to jump-start your style! Start by grouping your clothes together: Hang all pants together, skirts together, tops together, and dresses together. Then organize each type of clothing by length or sleeve-length and then by color, going from light to dark. Having a color-coded closet should make finding the right outfit a cinch!

> *A good mix: A warm overcoat for really cold days, a raincoat for the spring, and a less heavy coat like a light-wool gabardine or a simple cotton-cloth coat for fall and spring.*

Handle with Care ★ ★

Taking care of your clothes is as important as wearing them. Keeping them in like-new condition saves time and money (because you won't waste money and time shopping for items you've already bought but ruined because you didn't take proper care of them). Up next: Tips on how to store, wash, and repair your clothes.

Storing Your Clothes ★ ★ ★ ★ ★ ★ ★ ★ ★ ★ ★ ★

* Dry-cleaning—though it's obviously necessary!—also wears your clothes out quickly. So, after wearing an outfit you would normally dry-clean, lay your clothes on your bed and let them air out for about an hour before putting them away in your closet. This allows any odors clinging to your clothes to disperse. Generally, an outfit can be worn two or three times before dry-cleaning is necessary, but if your item seems in any way soiled or hard-worn, get it cleaned.

* Don't use wire hangers. They'll stretch out your clothes and can leave indentations in most fabrics that will have to be ironed or steamed out. Use thick, smooth wood or cedar hangers for heavier items such as wool or polyester jackets, blouses, and pants. Cedar hangers are thick and absorb moisture.

* Lightweight items, such as cotton blouses, dresses, and jackets, should be hung on wide, plastic hangers.
* Hang pants and skirts from the waist on pant hangers that have clips—this will keep them crease-free.
* Cotton sweaters and tees should be folded and put in drawers. Hanging will stretch them out.
* When it's spring and time to put away your warmer clothes, cashmere and wool sweaters should be folded and stored in plastic bags or boxes to keep moths out.
* Store leather items away from heat on strong wooden hangers. Don't wrap in plastic! Leather needs to breathe.

Style Secret:

Don't spray cologne directly onto your clothes—the alcohol in it can ruin the fabric. Be sure the cologne has dried on your skin—it only takes a sec!—before pulling on your garments, or spray carefully away from the fabric if you're already dressed.

Dry Clean, Hand Wash, or Tumble Dry? ★ ★ ★ ★ ★

Check the label to find out the best way to wash your garments.

If the tag says:	*Then:*
Dry Clean Only	Take the item to a dry-cleaner to get it professionally cleaned. Wool items will often fall in this category, as well as some delicate items, like blouses.
Hand Wash	Wash the item gently by hand, using a mild soap (check out the hand wash how-to on page 43).
Machine Wash Warm	Wash in the machine using warm water.
Machine Wash Cold	Wash in the machine using cold water.

Wash With Like Colors	Wash item only with similar colors, like whites with whites, or light colors with light colors.
No Bleach	Never use bleach. The fabric is probably too delicate.
Tumble Dry Low	Dry the item in the dryer using a low-heat setting.
Tumble Dry	Dry the item in the dryer using a regular-heat setting.
Dry Flat	Lay the item on a flat surface and let it air dry.
Line Dry	Hang the item on a clothes line or hanger to air dry.
Do Not Wring Dry	Don't squeeze and twist the item to get the excess water out. It could ruin the shape.

Hand Wash How-To:

Fabrics that are usually hand washed are delicate silks, knitted wool, fine linen, lace, and any clothing that has a decoration or design that could detach or fade in the washer. But since some of these items are dry-clean-only, always check the label first! You might want to ask your mom for help.

1. Dissolve one-teaspoon of gentle detergent, like Woolite, without bleach into COLD water—warm water can shrink your delicates!

2. Swish items through the water for a few minutes, rubbing gently if there are stains.

3. Don't wring dry—pat with a towel and then lay flat to dry, making sure to fluff the shape now and then.

4. If there are wrinkles, have your mom iron them with a light steam setting.

Fix It ★

* Most rips and tears will have to be sewn, so it's best to let your mom handle them.

* Don't let a rip or tear get out of control. If you don't repair it right away, it could end up getting much worse and ruining your fave sweater.

* You can use adhesive patches to cover up holes in jeans and other durable garments. They work like stickers—you just peel and stick. You can usually get patches at a craft or sewing store, and there are tons of designs to choose from.

Style Q & A

Q: I got a really short haircut at the beginning of the school year, and now I think all my clothes look weird on me. Is it just my imagination?

A: Probably not. After all, that's why people get haircuts—to change their look! However, "weird" is probably an exaggeration. What's most likely happening is that you were so used to seeing your clothes next to your old hair, that your new hair is making a distinct contrast. If your new hair's sporty and your old clothes were frilly, try switchin' those dresses for some more athletic looks and seeing if that makes a difference. Also, try to see this as an opportunity—after all, a short-haired you might be able to pull off some styles that wouldn't look nearly as cool with long hair!

Q: My mom says I can buy one really nice thing at the beginning of this school year. What's an awesome purchase that really has the most versatility for my wardrobe?

A: That's easy: A really cool bag, or a jacket, or a pair of shoes that are different from your everyday duds. Listen, you've got to have a sturdy backpack, a sensible coat, and shoes that last out the school year, right? The only problem is, that doesn't leave much room for individuality. But that's where this purchase comes in. Even if you don't wear it every day, a neon messenger bag, an awesome shearling jacket, or knee-high riding boots (just to give a few examples) can really become a signature item for you. If you think about it, you've probably got a favorite item you've seen on a friend or in a magazine that you've always thought would be cool to have. Go for it!

Q: How can I get the most out of my dressing time in the morning? I try to get up early, but I'm always sleeping past the alarm and throwing on anything from the heap in the corner. I'm sick of looking so sloppy!

A: Well, besides organizing your closet by style and color—it might take a few hours, but it'll save a lot of time later!—and stacking your jeans and tees so everything's neat and visible, there are some tried-and-true ways to avoid

that morning closet tizzy. First, the most easy one: Lay out your clothes the night before! Not only does this save you valuable time in the morning, it means your outfits will likely be better since you've really had time to look them over and think them through. Second, always do laundry regularly to keep that clean closet stocked! If your clothes are in a big junk heap, that's what you'll look like—and it puts a lot of wear and tear on your clothes when they're thrown around instead of stored properly. Bottom line? Take care of your clothes, and they'll take care of you!

5 RULES FOR THE ROAD

To get the most out of your clothes, always:

1. Follow the washing directions on the label

2. Buy hard-wearing fabrics for rough-'n-tumble tasks

3. Buy long-lasting, high-quality fabrics for standards like skirts, slacks, and coats

4. Store all your clothes in dry, clean areas (no, the floor doesn't count!)

5. Fix rips and tears promptly

Chapter 3

Shoes: Your Essential Accessory

Have you ever heard of aviators? Do you know whether to wear wedge or platform shoes when the weather gets warm? Well, it's time to take a walk on the wild side! Not only can shoes take a so-so outfit from drab to fab, they're a major consideration for any activity other than sitting on the couch (you don't want to wear hiking boots to a school dance any more than you want to try to scamper up a mountain in tennis shoes, right?). While it's true that your shoes take you from point A to point B, you need to be kind to your feet and help them feel and look awesome—as well as spunk up your overall look! So, before you lace up those sneaks, let's take a tour of the shoe department! You'll learn all you need to know about puttin' your best foot forward.

Taking Inventory ★ ★ ★ ★ ★ ★ ★ ★ ★ ★

Not sure why you need to know any more than which sneaks bounce the highest? Shoes are an important part of an outfit—in fact, some fashionistas think they're the most important part! Along with your awesome smile and eye-catching eyes, shoes are one of the first things people notice. They're also a great way to easily make an outfit fancy or casual—with just one change. So, check out this guide that includes all the styles you can sport!

Flats—Flat shoes have no heel height and are usually closed-toe. They look kind of like ballet slippers—and, not coincidentally, look great with flowy, sleek, dancer-type clothing.

Heels—Sounds obvious, right? Heels have a heightened heel. But there are a variety of different kinds:

⁂ **Pumps** are the most basic style, and are closed-toed. Pump heels can be fairly broad and low, or rather narrow and high. Something higher is great for a formal outfit, while a lower heel suits more casual, but nice outfits.

⁂ **Platforms** are really high and have either a tall square heel or a wedge heel, which looks like a wedge of cheese. You'll find platforms on  everything from boots to strappy sandals to sneaks. You can rock them in a casual way with khakis and denim, or add a playful twist to a sundress. The one time you'll never want to be in platforms? The icy winter...for—*whoops!*— obvious reasons.

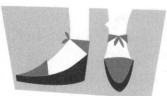

✳ **Kitten heels** are low pumps with a very narrow heel. They often have a narrow toe too, and look great with circle skirts and skinny jeans. Try a contrasting color, like bright red with blue jeans, for a really cute look!

Peep-toes—Peep-toes, or aviators, give a little peek-a-boo of the toes. These are the perfect kind of shoes to show off colorful nail polish in spring or summer—and accent a sundress or straight pencil skirt!

Sling-backs—Sling-backs have a strap around the ankle. They look great with fancier slacks and hose in the fall, or paired with simple dresses that echo their clean lines in the warmer months.

Mary-Janes—Mary-Janes look kind of like tap-dancing shoes, with a rounded toe, thick, square heel (either flat or tall), and a buckle strap over the bridge of the foot. They used to come in just black leather or patent leather, but now you can find them in tons of colors and materials—even sneaker-style! They give any look—except a lace dress, maybe—a fun, flirty edge.

Mules—Mules are closed-toe, slip-on shoes that are open in the back. They come in flats and heels, in everything from satin, wedge-heeled house-shoes to sneaker-front slides. You can find mules to match any outfit and style—just don't wear them when you need to run!

Slides—Slides are open-toed slip-ons—with a wide band over the bridge of the shoe. They can be casual or dressy, depending on the material, and they can look great with anything from a simple tank dress to jeans and a T-shirt.

Slip-ons—Slip-ons are closed-toe shoes without laces. These are a great shoe selection because they're so easy to take on and off, and are, generally, very comfortable. They come in tons of colors and shapes, from sleek black leather to high-tech vinyl with racing stripes! You can wear slip-ons with slightly more formal pants, or with everyday jeans.

Loafers—Loafers are business-style closed-toe shoes made of leather, often with a slot for a coin, which is why some styles are called "penny loafers." Wear these with slightly more formal pants or vintage jeans—save your sporty sneaks for your cargos and sweatshirts.

Oxfords—Oxfords are similar to loafers but lace up or buckle in the front. They look great with crisp blue jeans or wool pants.

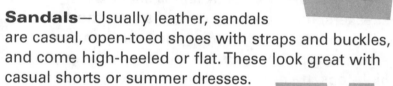

Sandals—Usually leather, sandals are casual, open-toed shoes with straps and buckles, and come high-heeled or flat. These look great with casual shorts or summer dresses.

Flip-flops—Also called thongs or shower shoes, flip-flops have thin straps that meet between the big and second toes. These shoes used to be the kind of rubber, casual summer shoe you'd only wear on the beach or in an outdoor shower. Nowadays, however, they come in all kinds of styles and colors, with platform soles, center flowers, rhinestones, and straps in velvet and other luxurious fabrics. While the traditional type is only for casual outfits, the fancier styles can be worn with dresses, bright Capris, flippy skirts, and other warm-weather wear.

Boots—A staple of winter, boots come in a variety of styles. There are:

✴ **Ankle boots,** which stop at your ankle. Great for bootcut pants or long, flowing skirts.

* **Knee boots**, which come up as high as your knee. Great with mini-skirts or bootcut jeans.
* **Cowboy boots**, which are western-style boots, usually come in black or brown suede, or hard leather, but they also come in all kinds of colors.

* **Combat or military boots** have a rounded toe, sturdy, wide, and thick soles, come to mid-calf, and lace up the front. They are heavy boots that can take you over the most difficult terrain, and they stand up to tough climates. Wear them with jeans and cargos.

Athletic shoes—AKA tennis shoes or sneakers, these come in tons of styles, most of which are designed to suit your heart-pumpin' activity of choice. There are slip-ons, lace-ups, high-tops, trainers, and low-tops. There are shoes

for basketball, baseball, soccer, running, tennis…as well as for pretty much any other sport you can think of! Materials are leather, suede, canvas, and cloth, with rubber soles. You don't want to mix up shoes specifically for one

sport with another—if you don't believe us, just try playing tennis in soccer cleats!

IN YOUR CLOSET

A good mix: One pair of closed-toe flats, one pair of casual shoes that aren't tennies— one pair of dressy shoes, a couple pairs of athletic shoes, and one pair of boots for rain or snow.

Put Your Best Foot Forward ★ ★ ★ ★ ★

Okay—now you know what mules are. But what the heck are you supposed to wear them with? Figuring out how to pair shoes with clothes can seem like a major stress-fest for the beginner or the shoe-phobic (if you've only got a pair of sneaks and one pair of "good" shoes in your closet, that's you!). But don't worry! There are a few simple rules to becoming a shoe-sensation, and once you get the hang of it, you'll be tapping your toes at how easy it can be. Just keep the following tips in mind the next time you head to your shoe rack.

✳ You can totally transform your look simply by changing your shoes. Swap sneaks for leather oxfords when wearing jeans or cargos, and transform a casual look into a dressy one—or style down your skirt by switching dress shoes for casual mules or low boots.

✳ Flats are best with skirts that are really long or really short. If you want some height with a long skirt or a mini, try chunky boots—they make a better contrast than pumps.

✳ Certain types of tennies can be paired with just about everything—even skirts and dresses. Colorful canvas sneakers work best. Be sure to pass on specific athletic shoes—like running shoes—and keep 'em for the sport they were intended.

✳ For a fun, casual, summertime look, try dressy flip-flops with sundresses. This look's great for pool parties and beach cookouts, too!

Style Secret: Sharing Shoes—NOT!

Don't share your shoes, even with your BFF. Letting someone else wear your sandals, tennies, or loafers can stretch them out so they no longer fit your feet. Everyone has a different walk. Plus, you could also get a—*ew!*—fungus.

What a Pair ★ ★ ★ ★ ★ ★ ★ ★ ★ ★ ★ ★ ★ ★ ★ ★

But what about more specific pairings? How do you know what shoes work best with Capris? With jeans? With skirts? Read on, shoe fly!

Jeans

So, what kind of shoes go best with jeans? It depends on the cut, but black flats create a classic, simple line and look good with any length jean. Other ideas:

* Bootcut and flare-leg jeans work best with knee boots, ankle boots, low-top tennies, mules, and heels—just make sure the hem of your pants reaches your ankle.

* Capri or cropped jeans are best with sandals, slides, flats, and low-top athletic shoes.

* Go for flats when wearing wide-legged jeans— sneakers look sloppy and heels look plain weird!

Pants Other Than Jeans

Basically, follow the same guidelines as for jeans, but with a few exceptions:

* Try loafers with cargos, wide-legged, and casual daytime trousers.

* Don't wear sneakers with dressy pants. Instead, opt for ankle boots or mules.

* Team cargo pants with sneakers; steer clear of strappy sandals, wedge, and kitten heels.

* Don't pair heels or ankle boots with Capris or cropped pants. Instead, try sandals, slides, flats, or kitten heels.

Skirts

Here are some skirt secrets for which shoes go best:

* Knee-high boots look fab with skirts, but make sure there's a bit of skin showing between the hem of the skirt and the top of the boot. Try not to pair ankle boots with short skirts—it shows too much skin and will give your body funny proportions. Save ankle

boots for pants and for pairing with flowy full-length skirts or dresses.

* Flirty circle skirts ooze Hollywood glamour when worn with flats. For the ultimate vintage look, try pairing a circle skirt with white tennies and short white socks—mega-1950s appeal!

* Pencil skirts look best with shoes that have a bit of height, like sling-backs or kitten heels.

* Wear casual jean skirts with slides or sandals. Want to dress up the look a bit? Try mules, kitten heels, or sling-backs.

Dresses

Check out these shoe tips for looking your best in a dress:

* Most dresses look best with pumps or ballet-style flats. If your dress is flowered cotton or has a certain cowgirl appeal, go with boots for a western look.

* Winter dresses, like sweater, wool, or long-sleeved shirt-dresses, can also be paired with knee boots. Just remember to keep a gap of skin showing between the top of the boot and the hem of the dress.

* Sundresses can be dressed up with flats, kitten heels, mules, and strappy sandals, or made casual with slides or cute flip-flops.

* Formal gowns should be worn with strappy sandals that have a bit of a heel, or Mary-Janes.

* Mules, loafers, or oxfords go best with simple, casual wool dresses or jumpers.

Shoe IQ ★ ★ ★ ★ ★ ★ ★ ★ ★ ★ ★ ★ ★ ★ ★

You wear them all the time, but do you know what material your shoes are made of? Most shoes are made of leather, like:

* **suede**, which is soft and nubby. Dress shoes, boots, loafers, and some slides come in suede. Suede looks soft and gorgeous, but it stains easily and can be difficult to clean.

* **smooth leather**, which can be either soft and delicate, or hard with a matte finish, which lasts longer and is better for the outdoors. Leather shoes are everywhere—including your shmancy sneakers!

* **patent leather**, which is hard and shiny (your little sis probably wears patent leather dress-up shoes). Patent leather can be found on dress shoes, loafers, Mary-Janes—any shoe that looks great with a shine!

But there are also a ton of other shoe materials, including:

* **vinyl**, which can look like patent leather or leather, in which case it's called "pleather." You'll see this on loafers, boots, and all kinds of summer shoes, since it's lighter than leather.

* **canvas**, which is a cloth fabric and is usually used for athletic shoes.

Stylin' Shoe Shades ★ ★ ★ ★ ★ ★ ★ ★ ★ ★ ★ ★

So, you've got your styles, materials, and pairings down, but we haven't discussed the most important thing: Color! Shade is a super-important element to consider when choosing the right pair of shoes—a splash of color on your slides can make your outfit *zing* or create a chaotic clash. Read on for tips on giving your shoes and outfits major matching appeal.

* Snazz up a monochromatic (one-color) look with a pair of bright shoes. While you want to keep your shoe color similar to the rest of your outfit, make sure it isn't an exact match (unless you're talking black, brown, navy, beige, or white). You want it to complement the shade. If you're unsure, wear or bring the clothing item to the shoe store and take a second look.

* Keep away from black shoes when wearing a white outfit. The contrast is too drastic. And vice versa.

* Instead of bright white shoes, choose off-white or cream. White can make your feet look bigger than they are, and they get dirty easily. Save white for sneaks and canvas slides or mules.

* Pair camel or tan shoes with navy pants. Neutral-colored shoes, like beiges, also work well with dark blue, and you'll want to match your socks, tights, or hose (neutral with neutral, black with black) with your shoes for a clean line.

Try This On for Size ✶ ✶ ✶ ✶ ✶ ✶ ✶ ✶ ✶ ✶ ✶ ✶

It's important that your shoes fit perfectly. Besides being uncomfortable, shoes that don't fit well can cause blisters, corns, or more serious injuries, like breaks or sprains. Think about it: If your foot isn't properly supported, you're more prone to trip or fall. Wearing super-tall heels isn't worth a sprained ankle or broken arm—especially if it happens in front of the whole school at a dressy event!

To find your shoe size, shoe stores have special devices that measure the size of your feet. You've probably been sized a gazillion times, right? Get used to it: Until you completely finish growing, your feet will keep changing size and shape.

Once your foot becomes a size 4 or higher, you can wear women's shoes as well as girls' shoes. A girls' size 5-1/2 is usually equal to a women's size 4. But the very best way to get a feel for how a pair of shoes will fit is obvious—try them on!

Here are nine great shoe-shopping tips:

1. Whenever you try on shoes, bring a pair of socks with you. You need to see how the shoe will fit with socks—plus, this keeps your feet clean. Just be sure to match your socks to the footwear: Bring

heavier socks when trying on boots, regular or trouser socks for oxfords and loafers, tube socks for sneakers, and peds (or hosiery mini-socks) for fancy, slim footwear.

2. Try both shoes on and walk around in them. Make sure there's a half-inch of breathing room between your big toe and the hood of the shoe.

3. Never buy shoes that are too tight. Ever. They will always be uncomfortable—probably so uncomfortable you'll barely be able to walk after a day of wearing them. Instead, try the next half size or size up. If that pair's too big, it's better to pass and go for another style shoe—your feet and those shoes simply weren't meant for each other!

4. Also, watch out for sandals or shoes with straps that are tight around your ankle or dig into your skin. Ouch!

5. Be careful with flip-flops with heels. The angle of the shoe can make your foot slide forward, putting extra pressure (and pain) on the toes.

6. Nix heels that are too high. It'll be difficult to keep your balance in them, and hard to walk—and keep up with your friends! Opt for lower kitten heels instead, which have a girlie, glam look and are better for your feet.

7. Shoes made from synthetic material—like vinyl, plastic, and pleather—make feet sweat, which will wear out your shoes faster and make your shoes smell. Leather, suede, and canvas let feet breathe and are more durable. Even if they're more expensive, they're worth it—they last much, much longer.

8. Shop for shoes at the end of the day rather than the beginning—your feet swell later in the day, and shoes that fit then will also fit in the AM. If you shop for shoes in the morning, the same pair may pinch you at night.

9. If you're wearing a new pair of hard-soled shoes for the first time, find a sidewalk or another rough surface and scuff the soles up a bit. Be careful: New shoes can be very slippery on smooth surfaces like wooden floors and stairs!

Shoe Shape-Up ★ ★ ★ ★ ★ ★

Like your clothes, your shoes need TLC. Taking good care of them means they'll look better and last longer—and that you'll be able to style in them happily for years to come! So, get under the bed and yank those puppies out from between the dust bunnies—it's time to organize!

Storage

The very best way to keep your shoes in shape is to store them on a shoe-tree. If you have room in your closet, another alternative is to keep shoes in

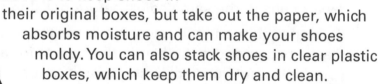

their original boxes, but take out the paper, which absorbs moisture and can make your shoes moldy. You can also stack shoes in clear plastic boxes, which keep them dry and clean.

Keep the shoes you wear all the time in front—that way they're right there when you need them. We know, it's easier said than done, but don't throw your shoes in a pile—not only is it hard to see everything, but regular rummaging through the shoe pile will make your shoes scuffed and worn.

Care

Here's the number one way to keep your shoes in tip-top shape: Don't wear the same pair every single day! Everybody's feet sweat, and foot perspiration makes shoes wear out quickly. If you rotate pairs and wear a different one each day, you'll save them from getting a lethal case of the moldies.

Also, even though it's tempting, NEVER dry your shoes on a heater or in front of a fireplace. The extreme heat can make rubber melt and leather stiffen. The best thing to do is to take the insoles out and let both the shoes and the insoles air-dry in a cool, moisture-free place, or in front of a fan.

Cleaning Tips

Regular cleaning and polishing will keep your tappers in tune. Here are some easy-to-follow steps to making your shoes shine:

* Wipe off loose dirt with a damp cloth. If your shoes have water stains, you'll need to use a special shoe cleaner that removes the stains.

* If your white shoes have scuffs, fill in the marks with white-out and then polish them. Scuff marks on black or colored shoes can be covered up with acrylic paints, permanent markers, or paint-repair pens of the same color, before polishing.

* If you get gum on your fave pair, cover them completely in a plastic bag and toss the bag in the freezer for a few hours— you don't want your gross shoes next to food. Gum is easier to scrape off when it's frozen. (Tip: Warn the cook of the house before throwing anything in the fridge!)

* To make a buckle sparkle, scrub it with an old toothbrush and toothpaste, and then wipe it off with a damp rag. It should shimmer like new!

* The best way to keep athletic shoes in shape is to spray them with a water and stain repellent when you first buy them. When cleaning, you can either wash shoes with a special shoe shampoo, or you can use a little rubbing alcohol on cotton balls and gently rub shoes clean. Be sure to take out laces and clean those by hand in soapy water. Don't put shoes in the washing

machine, unless tags specify that it's OK. Let shoes air-dry in a cool, moisture-free area. Keep away from heat!

✻ Leather shoes need to be polished every few months. Use a cream polish for soft leather and wax polish for hard leather. You can find shoe polish at most drug stores.

✻ Brush suede lightly with sandpaper and then protect your shoes with a shoe-protecting spray, which you can buy at a shoe store.

✻ Have a pair of super stinky sneaks? Pour a little baking soda in the bottom and let them air out overnight. Then wipe out the soda with a lightly damp paper towel.

Style Secret: What is a foot fungus?

Athlete's foot is a fungal infection that affects the skin, making it dry, flakey and itchy. People whose feet sweat a lot are more prone to infection, but you can do a few things to protect your tootsies:

- To prevent athlete's foot, don't share your shoes.
- Wear flip-flops when hanging out at public pools—especially in the locker room.
- Make sure your toenails are kept short and trimmed straight across.
- Change your shoes often, and throw out smelly, moldy tennies.
- Dry your feet well after showering.
- Don't wear oxfords, sneakers, or other full-foot shoes without socks.

Repair

Don't toss those sandals out just because the soles have worn down! Here are some things you should know about repairing your shoes:

✻ If you have holes in the soles of your shoes, or your heels have worn out, take them to a shoe repair shop. The shoemaker can put in new soles or add new heels—making your shoes almost as good as new.

✻ A shoe repair shop can replace worn out buckles, straps, and eyelets—the metal rivets that hold your laces—as well.

✻ If the lining of your shoe comes out, glue it back in with rubber cement; this fix you can do yourself.

Shoe Q & A

Q: My sister says that if I wear shoes that are too small, I will have deformed feet when I grow up. She's just trying to scare me, right?

A: "Deformed" may be taking things a bit far, but your sis *is* telling you the truth: Tight shoes cause major problems! Shoes that don't fit properly can lead to—*ugh!*—bunions, corns, blisters, ingrown toenails, mashed toes, and many other foot nightmares that you never want to see, as well as contribute to backaches, leg pain, and—duh!—foot pain. Want your feet to stay healthy, grow properly, and do the work of supporting your spine that they're made for? Then always—ALWAYS!—buy shoes that are comfortable and give your feet room to breathe. Your healthy feet will thank you!

Q: I don't have enough room in my closet to store all my shoes, so I put my winter shoes in the attic in the summer, and vice versa. The only problem is, when I make my switch, they're all dusty and cracked! How can I store them so they stay in shape for next season?

A: Overly dry air can crack the material of your shoes, overly damp air can make them—ew!—moldy, and dust can permanently stain and destroy the color. Leaving shoes in a big, yucky heap can also permanently mess up the shape! So, how do you make sure that your stored-away shoes stay in trim? First of all, make sure that the area you've chosen is clean and dry—not too close to any radiators or other heating elements, and far, far away from damp spots like concrete basement floors or sinks. Next, take each pair of shoes and, using crumpled up scrap paper, brown paper bags, or newspaper, firmly fill them out—this will help them retain their shape. While shoeboxes are best for shoe storage, if you haven't had time to save up a bunch, plastic boxes or even clean paper bags will do in a pinch. Place your shoes in neat heel-to-toe pairs, and don't stack shoes directly on top of one another—place firm cardboard or something rigid between pairs to make sure they don't smush. A little care and prevention should keep your shoes stylin' until the seasons change.

Q: If you wear open-toed shoes, does your toenail polish have to match?

A: Matching your polish is always a nice look for a really formal outfit, but it's not necessary for everyday looks—and slickin' it on regularly is pretty time-consuming, too! Toenails that are neatly trimmed and buffed look nice with any sandal, and clear or neutral polish matches any outfit. To complete your look, after you've gotten your toenails in order, moisturize your feet and sprinkle a little powder on the soles to keep your feet lookin' and smellin' dandy in slides or sandals too.

Q: In the summer, my family does a lot of outdoor water sports like kayaking, creek-walking, and sailing. I usually just wear an old pair of tennis shoes, but they get so moldy and gross by the end of the summer! Is there anything I can do to make them hold up better?

A: If you constantly dip your shoes in muddy water, they're going to get moldy—you'd have to wash them in ammonia after every outing to prevent it! A better option is to invest in a pair of shoes that are designed for wet/dry walking or outdoor activities. Look for sneaker-type soles with a synthetic mesh top, or shoes with "aqua" or "wet/dry" worked into the name. These shoes are built to keep your feet stable and safe, like your tennies, but they dry out quickly and are specially treated to prevent mold or other nasty crud from growing inside. They'll also let you save your tennies for what they're designed for—tennis!

Q: I really love the cute, clunky boots everyone's rockin', but I'm really tall for my age. Are there any shoes in this style I can wear, or do I just have to wear flat shoes?

A: You may feel the need to try and be shorter because you're taller than most of your friends, but try not to let it bother you. (Hey, think of it this way: To be a supermodel or successful volleyball or B-ball player, you have to be tall!) In short, wear any kind of boot that you like—tall people don't need to stick to flats. If you can't seem to do it and want a shoe that doesn't pack as much height, go for slides that have a slight heel. But, honestly, be proud of the fact that you stand out in the crowd!

Q: My closet is a mess. Have any tips to help me organize my shoes?

A: Keeping shoes neat and tidy will make getting dressed way easier. To kick off a more organized shoe collection, first get rid of any shoes that no longer fit or that you just don't wear anymore. Next, figure out how you'll store the shoes you do keep—in a metal shoe rack, stacked on individual shelves, or in canvas shoe bags, in clear plastic boxes, or in the original boxes. Keep the shoes you wear most often within easy reach. You might opt to keep casual shoes on the rack and more formal shoes in boxes. If you do keep shoes in the original boxes, tape pictures of the shoes to the outside. You can do this by taking Polaroids or digital pics that you print out on your printer and attach to the side of the box facing you. This way, you'll be more likely to wear shoes you remember you have!

5 RULES FOR THE ROAD

Proper footwear care's a shoe-in! Just be sure to...

1. Never wear shoes that are too tight or way too loose—no matter how cute!

2. Never put rubber-soled shoes in the dryer

3. Always store shoes separately and neatly in clean, dry boxes, or shoe boxes

4. Always toss shoes that are beyond stinky salvation

5. Always test drive your new shoes by scuffing up the soles on a rough surface so you don't slip when you wear them

Chapter 4

Getting Dressed

So, you've got your closet organized, and you've got the basics down. But how do you mix up all your tees, jeans, and shoes when you're ready to go from standard to standout? And what are some sassy separates to help spice up an outfit? Read on for some wardrobe do's and don'ts that will help you always know the right thing to wear—no matter where you're going!

Mix 'n' Match ★ ★ ★ ★ ★ ★ ★ ★ ★ ★ ★

Putting together the right outfit can seem tricky, but now that you're armed with smarts about crewnecks, cardigans, boot-legged jeans, and shoes, it's time to turn that know-how into superstar looks.

Jeans from A to Z ★ ★ ★ ★ ★ ★ ★ ★ ★ ★ ★ ★

Try these fun jean looks:

Sporty Prep: Medium-colored jeans, a gray polo or baseball-style shirt, canvas belt, and tennies.

College Girl: Light-colored jeans with a white tee or polo, a soft cardigan, and penny loafers.

Retro: Dark jeans, shimmery tank-top, chain belt, and platforms.

Sailor Girl: Wide-legged dark jeans with a striped boatneck shirt and canvas sneakers.

✳ **Night and Day:** During the day, try a pair of dark jeans with a simple white tee under a V-neck or crewneck sweater with boots. Once the sun goes down, swap the tee and sweater for a flutter-sleeve blouse and change into kitten heels. Or, keep the tee on and throw a blazer on over it.

✳ **All denim:** You can do jeans and a jacket, a vest and a circle skirt, a denim blazer and a mini—but be sure of two things: 1) that the washes vary in color, and 2) you steer clear of a totally flat dye in your denim. You want a denim look, not a denim uniform!

Style Secret: History of Jeans

Believe it or not, jeans have been around for over 100 years. In 1853, during the California gold rush, a tailor named Levi Strauss created the first pair after one of his customers, a miner, complained that his pants were always ripping. Strauss had a supply of strong, brown canvas cloth, which he had planned to use for tents and wagon covers. Instead, he used the material for the pants, which sported front and back pockets, a button fly, and reinforced stitching. Strauss sold his pants for—get this—22¢ a pair! They flew off his shelves. Eventually, Strauss swapped the brown canvas for blue denim, added metal rivets to make them even stronger, and patented his pants in 1873. In 1890, they were named "501," which happened to be the lot number assigned to that leather patch you still see on the back. They weren't called "501s" by the public until the 1960s, when wearing jeans really picked up speed and became not only a standard American but an international look as well. The look of 501s is virtually unchanged from 1873, except for the addition of belt loops. It's possible you might be wearing the same kind of jeans your great-, great-, great-grandfather wore!

Fashion Fun: Layering Tees ★ ★ ★ ★ ★ ★ ★ ★ ★ ★

You can create a fun look by layering tees and tank tops. Try these combinations:

Tee over tank top: Mix up your colors and styles—hint of pink, anyone?—or stick with neutrals for a suave peek-a-boo look.

Round-neck tee over long-sleeved tee: Make sure the collar of the shirt underneath doesn't show with this combo.

Scoop-neck tee with long bell sleeves over tank: Don't want to wear the world on your shoulders? This look lets you get the scoop without falling into it.

Low V-neck tee over tank: Feeling like you're in too deep? Don't sweat the V—stick a tank underneath and you won't feel like a square.

One-color (Monochromatic) Color Schemes ★ ★ ★ ★

As you've already found out, a monochromatic color scheme means wearing one-color from head to toe. Monochrome outfits pair pieces and accessories that are in the same color family, but vary by shade—like all off-yellows, all pinks, or all blues. Although the mono look goes in and out of fashion, it's definitely a classic combo, and lots of celeb stylists recommend it to give the bod a clean, slimmer, taller line.

In order to put together a monochromatic, or one-color outfit, you'll want to blend, mixing pieces that are lighter and darker shades of a color. For example:

✳ **To create a YELLOW monochrome color scheme,**
you could mix pale yellow, white, and cream.

✳ **To create an ORANGE scheme,**
you could mix tan, pumpkin, and coral.

✳ **To create a PINK scheme,**
you could mix pale pink, hot pink, and light red.

✳ **To create a RED scheme,**
you could mix dark brown, rusty orange, and brick red.

✳ **To create a PURPLE scheme,**
you could mix violet, lavender, and eggplant.

* **To create a GREEN scheme,**
  you could mix olive, pale green, and dark green.

* **To create a BLUE scheme,**
  you could mix navy, slate blue, and pale blue.

* **To create a BROWN scheme,**
  you could mix chocolate, camel, and beige.

* **To create a GRAY scheme,**
  you could mix charcoal, slate, and light gray.

* **To create a BLACK scheme,**
  you could mix dark black with charcoal.

What Do I Wear To...? ★ ★ ★ ★ ★ ★ ★ ★

Okay, so you "get" monochromatic color schemes. You know what kinds of shoes to wear with jeans. And you even understand how to layer tees. But having the wardrobe wisdom needed to choose the right outfit for every occasion takes practice and experience—and a lot of style savvy! Feast your eyes on the following best bets for school, parties, family gatherings, wintertime, and more.

School ★ ★ ★ ★ ★ ★ ★

Hey, you spend a lot of time in the classroom, so your school wardrobe should definitely be comfortable. Still, that doesn't mean slumming to school in sweatpants! Save sweatsuits for the gym or weekends. Those fuzzy velour numbers included.

School Style Do's:

- **Cargo pants**
- **Capris or cropped pants**
- **Wide-leg/sailor pants, or jeans**
- **Corduroy pants**

- Flare-leg or boot-cut jeans
- Pencil skirts
- A-line skirts
- T-shirts in various styles
- Button-up blouses
- Sweaters of all cuts and styles
- Zip-up sweatshirts (minus those, uh, matchin' pants!)

- Blazers or vintage style jackets
- Shirtdresses
- Sundresses—but only with sweaters over them
- Clean sneakers (not beaten-up, weekend sneaks)
- Oxfords
- Flats

School Style No-Nos:

- Tank tops, unless worn as a layer under tees, or topped with a sweater or zip-up sweatshirt
- Micro-minis (A bit above the knee is fine for school—but not much more!)

- Shorts
- Sweatpants and sweatshirts, except during gym
- Heels that are too high, like spikes or three-inch pumps

Hallway Hall of Fame

You're sure you don't want to rock a pink boa and platform lizard boots, but that doesn't mean you wouldn't mind standing out... in a good way. Based on your personal style file, here are four outfits that will always mean you rule the school.

* **Classic:** Slip into an A-line skirt with a polo tee, cardigan, and flats. Put it all together in a monochrome color scheme, like neutrals, charcoals, or—if you're feelin' sassy—pinks! You can dress it up with simple jewelry, like tiny pearl earrings or small hoops, and a charm bracelet.

* **Modern:** Rock some dark, skinny jeans with layered tees and ballet flats. Smooth your hair back in a low pony or add a fabric headband to the look. Mix with studs or stiletto (slim, straight-line) earrings.

* **Girly:** Try a slim dress with a button-up sweater and sling-backs. Go for teardrop earrings and a vintage watch.

* **Sporty:** Pull on cargo pants with a cap-sleeve tee and sneaker-slides. Chilly? Add a zip-up jacket and a block-striped scarf. You don't need jewelry—a high pony should do the job.

Blaze a New Trail

Whether you're doing an oral report for History or running for student council, sometimes you need people at school to pay attention and take you seriously. Looking professional will grab their attention, so go for a semi-business look by wearing a blue or black blazer. A blazer is one of those amazing items that can look great with a variety of styles, while still maintaining that "In 1492, Columbus sailed the ocean blue" vibe you're going for.

So, add some funk by pairing dark jeans with the blazer, or get retro and pull your hair back with a wide-scarf headband and don hoop earrings. Want to be more girly? Wear a fluttery blouse under a bright blazer, or, if you're on the sporty side, wear a plain tee. You can even match the blazer to a skirt and wear pumps, but don't be surprised if your classmates think you took a wrong turn on your way to Wall Street!

Uniforms

If you go to a school that requires you to wear uniforms, you probably have limited wiggle room in terms of what you can wear to school. Instead of bumming, add cool accessories. Try:

* Wearing a funky beaded cardigan over your uniform.
* Jazzing up your shirt or sweater by sporting a rhinestone brooch.
* Sporting fun barrettes or headbands in your hair.
* Wearing bright-colored knee socks or tights.
* Tying a cool scarf around your neck in the same colors as your skirt. Or if your uniform is solid, go for a scarf with bold patterns in complementing colors.

- Adding a funky belt—a cool studded one, 1970s disco chain, or 1980s-style wide belt, or wrap a long scarf around your waist.
- Donning a fuzzy winter wool scarf in a bright color.
- Sporting a newsboy cap, a beret, or a knit stocking cap over braids.

Parties ★ ★ ★ ★ ★ ★ ★ ★ ★ ★ ★ ★ ★ ★ ★

Family gatherings, birthdays, dances. So many parties, so little time! And so little time to figure out what to wear. Well, don't worry—there's rules for this kind of stuff, and the time of year and the kind of party you've been invited to will determine what you should wear. (Still leaving room for you to express your individual style, of course!) Do you know when to go floor-length and when jeans will do? Read on to find out.

- **Formal:** If you've got a wedding or a formal event to attend, it means you should dress up. A nice cocktail (that means knee-length, but still dressy) dress and a pretty wrap with heels or Mary-Janes should do.

- **Dress Casual/Informal:** Go for nice trousers, cargo pants, wide-legged, sailor pants, or skirts with sweaters, button-ups, or blouses. A fluttery sundress is good in warm weather; a corduroy skirt and nubbly sweater is great when it's cold.

- **Casual:** This means you're free to dress as you please. Jeans and tees are A-OK with this dress code.

Family Gatherings & Holidays ★ ★ ★ ★ ★ ★ ★ ★ ★ ★

Fall/Winter

The chilly season is chock-full of
parties and family gatherings. 'Tis
the season to let your style sparkle.
Holiday colors are bold and bright
reds, greens, blues, silvers, and golds.
Fabrics are shiny and fuzzy—velvets,

feathers, faux fur, velour, and cashmere. Check out
these sizzlin' suggestions for festive holiday looks.

* **Classic:** Black velvet dress with black Mary-Janes and a fun
  faux fur wrap.
* **Modern:** Red pencil skirt, red boat-neck sweater, rhinestone
  belt, flats, and a fuzzy red boa-style scarf.
* **Girlie:** Below-knee A-line skirt in a soft material, paired with
  a sparkly silver tank, and Mary-Janes.
* **Sporty:** Dark blue satin (or satin-like) wide-leg pants, a
  velvet wrap-top, and flats.

Spring/Summer

Warm-weather holidays and gatherings kick off the season of spring
picnics and hikes. It's getting warmer, the sun's out, and spring invites
pastel colors and lighter clothes like khakis, light sweaters, and tees,
while summer brings in a tropical palette in thin, airy cottons and
linens. Read on for spring and summer's best looks!

* **Classic:** For spring, try khaki Capris, a pastel tee with a light
  cardigan or jean jacket, black or brown leather sandals. In
  summer, try a white linen dress, the same sandals, and a
  thin wrap. Wear tiny silver hoop earrings for that extra touch.
* **Modern:** Jean mini-skirts are great for both spring and
  summer—just add a pastel, funky blouse with mules (for
  spring), or layered monochrome tank tops with bright-colored
  slides (for summer).
* **Girlie:** For spring weather, slip into a long khaki skirt and a
  linen blouse, with casual mules. For summer days, jump into
  a flowery sundress with casual sandals.

✳ **Sporty:** Put on a pretty cap-sleeved tee, bright-white sneaks and crisp white socks, pairing it with either a stretchy wrap tennis skirt or shorts in the summer, or light cargos or Capris in the spring. Don't forget your shades!

Working Out ★ ★ ★ ★ ★ ★ ★ ★

'Kay, sporty girl—here is where your style shines. Wear sweatpants and tees for working out, or for practice. If it's summer, you can swap pants for shorts, with a tee on top. Most important, make sure your shoes are comfortable when running, jumping, and sliding. And keep those workout clothes fresh and clean, too!

Four Season Fashion ★ ★ ★ ★ ★ ★ ★

Ah, the smell of spring! The chill of winter! The flurries of fall and the heat waves of summer! With all these temperature changes, how's a gal to keep cool? Read on for fashion faves for each seasonal sitch!

1) Winter Checklist

Brrr! Trying to stay stylish and warm can be tough, but you're sure to be toasty with *GL*'s winter wisdom. Layering is a cold-weather must. Long-sleeved cotton tees or thermals over a short-sleeved tee are a

perfect start. Then, try a zip-up sweater and parka-style vest. Or go for a snuggly winter coat over the sweater. Wrap a scarf around your neck and you've got instant winter glam! Wool pants or corduroys are best on the bottom, and boots are a snazzy way to keep your feet warm. If you live in a warmer climate, you can ditch heavier coats and go for blazers, windbreakers or jean jackets. Here's a checklist of some basic winter items you should have in your wardrobe:

- Scarf
- Gloves
- Boots
- Longer skirts
- Parka
- Ski vest
- Thermals
- Raincoat (with lining)

- Winter coat
- Sweaters
- Long-sleeved tees
- Zip-up sweatshirts
- Socks
- Tights
- Red, green, blue, silver and black are some winter colors

Winter Fabrics

To keep you warm, wintertime fabrics need to be strong and durable, like:

Wool   Tweed   Corduroy

Or fun, like

Faux Fur   Satin   Velvet

2) Spring Checklist

The icicles have melted, flowers are in bloom, and the sun is starting to peek out. Springtime means your wardrobe can loosen up—and colors can get brighter. Layering is still an important style choice in spring, since the temperature can still be chilly. Keep a sweater or light jacket with you. Here are some basic springtime pieces:

- Light jacket
- 3/4-length tees
- Hooded sweatshirts
- Button-up sweaters
- Medium-color jeans

- Capri pants later in spring
- Flats
- Sneakers
- Socks
- Tights

Spring Fabrics

Time to stow the wool away until next winter and get out into the sometimes warm, sometimes chilly spring air! Because the temps are changing, spring fabrics are light, cool, and breathable, like:

Cotton   **Linen**   **Washable silk**

3) Summer Checklist

It's hot. Days are longer. And you're probably spending loads of time outdoors. Besides making sure your bod is coated in a thick layer of sunscreen, summer style is all about comfort and simplicity. Shorts and tees are standard summer gear, but try mixing up your casual look with light cotton skirts, jean skirts, or sundresses. You can still pair those items with tennies, but also with mules, slides, or strappy sandals. Check your closet for these summer must-haves:

- **Shorts of various lengths and styles**
- **Jean skirt**
- **Light cotton skirt**
- **Tank tops in various colors**

- **Short-sleeved or sleeveless tees**
- **Cute flip-flops**
- **Sandals**
- **Bathing suit**
- **Sunglasses**

Summer Fabrics

Light and airy fabrics will help you stay cool in the season of not-so-cool weather. Try:

Canvas   **Cotton**   **Woven straw (good for sandals)**

4) Fall Checklist

Summer is over. The days are getting shorter—and cooler. Pull out those light-weight wool sweaters, and go back to layering. A fall wardrobe could include:

- 3/4-inch tees
- Long-sleeved button-up
- Blouse
- Long jeans
- Sailor pants
- Pull-over sweater
- Cardigan sweater
- Zip-up sweatshirt
- Long-sleeved dress
- Leather jacket

- Blazer
- Ankle boots
- Knee boots
- Loafers or slip-ons
- Oxfords
- Closed-toe flats
- Scarf

Fall Fabrics

To keep warm through school and those chillier days, check out:

Light-weight Wool   **Silk**   **Leather**

Style Q & A

Q: I live in a pretty warm climate. What are my clothing options for school?

A: Lucky you! Well, gals in warm climates don't need to load up on the wool and suede boots—and they can go positively crazy with cotton, linen, and washable silk! A great mix for all-over warm-weather fun is two or three sundresses (you can go sleek and modern, short and sporty, or flowery and frilly—or get one of each), three skirts (try to get a knee-length, one above-the-knee, and one longer skirt to encompass all looks), a nice mix of tees and light blouses in your fave colors, and some Capris.

Q: In school pictures, the backgrounds are always ugly. Should I try to match it or stand out? All I know is that I want to look totally great this year!

A: Looking great in school pictures can be pretty tough, but with a little planning ahead, you can do it! It's best to choose something that is most flattering to you. Also, stay away from bold colors—you're more likely to clash with the background. Choosing more neutral colors, white or off-white (though it's a little plain), or a lighter shade of a color, is your best bet. And lastly, stay away from busy designs or stripes—you want the camera to focus on your pretty face!

Q: I'm an athlete, and I hardly have any time to get ready after morning and afternoon practice. I usually stick with jeans, sneakers, and sweatshirts or T-shirts outside the locker room, but I'm getting sick of my boring look. What are some quick outfits I can put together to spice it up?

A: Since you're going to be folding these up and sticking them in a bag, you'll need to concentrate on wrinkle-free separates that are easy to shake out and shimmy into. Polyester blend skirts and tops are awesome for you—these separates not only look great on, they'll stay in shape even crumpled in your sports bag! For cold weather, try mixing these with a long sweater-jacket, leather Mary-Janes, and colored tights. For warm weather, simply throw on some matching slides. Adding simple, easily carried jewelry, like small studs or a charm bracelet, can take the look even further. You should be stylin' out of gym wear in no time!

5 RULES FOR THE ROAD

To select the best outfits, always...

1. Lay out your clothes the night before. It saves time and you'll be more likely to wind up wearing a matching outfit!

2. Try to build up a wardrobe of versatile, go-together items. Before you buy something, hold it up: Does it go with something you already have?

3. Clean out your closet seasonally and rearrange your clothes to make it easy to grab your Capris in the summer and your wool pants in the winter.

4. Get colorful: Find your best colors and keep a note of them! This will make shopping—and getting dressed in the morning—much easier.

5. Match fabrics to seasons: You might love those linen pants, but unless you live in Hawaii, December is no time to be wearing 'em.

Chapter 5

Smashin' Fashion You Can Do Yourself

You don't have to buy your entire wardrobe at the mall! Not only can you save a little dough by making your own accessories, you can totally customize your look and have fun doing it! There are tons of fun things you can make yourself—or with your pals. All you need is a little creativity and some inspiration. In this chapter, you'll find some recipes for DIY fashion that will leave you looking fabulous!

Salvage Chic ★ ★ ★ ★ ★ ★ ★ ★ ★ ★ ★ ★

Getting ready to toss those old jeans? Wait! Before you send them off to Goodwill, consider turning them into recycled fashion. Often, designers use old clothes to create trendy new pieces with just a few simple modifications or embellishments. Read on and you, too, can become a design diva.

Jazzy Jeans

Pop-star inspired jeans with rhinestones, patches, and beads don't have to cost a fortune. With a few inexpensive details, you can sport celeb-style jeans created by this year's hottest new designer—you!

Supplies:

- **Your fave pair of jeans**
- **Fabric marker**
- **Fabric glue**
- **Depending on the design you choose, you'll need decorative embellishments, all of which can be found at a craft store: Assorted beads, rhinestones, buttons, fabric paints, glitter, adhesive patches, ribbon, funky fabrics**

Difficulty Level: Super Simple

What you do:

How you decorate your jeans is up to you. You can go as outrageous as you dare. Here are some suggestions:

1. Using a fabric marker, outline some designs and then use fabric glue to adhere beads, rhinestones, or buttons along the lines of your design.
2. You can create designs with fabric paint and fill in the outlined areas with glitter. Spread a light layer of fabric glue inside the fabric-painted design and then sprinkle glitter onto the glue. Wait 24 hours before wearing 'em.

3. Try gluing buttons or rhinestones around the seams of pockets for a smaller, decorative look.

4. Stick an adhesive flower or butterfly patch to one of your back pockets.

5. You can trim your jean hems with ribbon or fabric, creating colorful cuffs. Attach fabric or ribbon using your fabric glue.

Remember: When caring for your hand-embellished jeans, your best bet is to hand-wash them so none of the decorations come off. If you know they're attached fairly securely (or you're willing to risk it), turn the jeans inside out before putting them in the washing machine.

From Pants to Capris

You can give retro style to old pants by transforming them into Capris.

Supplies:
- **One pair of old pants or jeans**
- **Pen**
- **Ruler**
- **Scissors**

Step 1

Difficulty Level: Super Simple

What you do:

1. Try your pants or jeans on and consider how short you want to make them. Once you decide, mark the inside of the pant leg with the pen at the length where you want it to end. Capris usually end mid- to lower-calf.

2. Lay the pants on a flat surface. Find the pen mark. Using a ruler, draw a line from the pen mark across the pant leg. Do this on both legs. Make sure the line is straight all the way around on each pant leg.

Step 2

3. Cut along the line, trying to keep it as straight as possible. Then, you're done! Just pair your new Capris with a vintage sweater for a look straight from the 1950s!

Step 3

Four Things You Can Do with a Plain White T-Shirt

Here are a bunch of funky looks using one classic, white tee.

1. Graffi-tee

Get crafty and give your tee a custom flavor.

Supplies:

- **T-shirt**
- **Markers (Tip: Make sure your markers are not water-soluble—they should say "permanent". Test them by coloring a small patch of the fabric you want to use. Let your mark dry for a minute or so, and then rinse it under a faucet. If it doesn't run, you're good to go!)**
- **Scissors**

Difficulty Level: Super Simple

What you do:

What you draw and design on your tee is up to you, but here are some funky ideas:

* Get punked with colored permanent markers to spread your message. Use black, green, orange, purple, and red—mix it up!

* Draw racing stripes down the side seams for a subtle detail.

✷ Trim off the sleeves (making your tee a tank). Then, run the side of the marker tip along the newly cut edges. This will add a splash of color to your tee.

✷ Write a message that means something to you and your friends along the hem, around the collar, or up the side seam.

2. Trim the Edges!

Here's a sassy look that will get your friends talking!

Supplies:
- **T-shirt**
- **Scissors**

Step 1

Difficulty Level: Super Simple

What you do:

1. Use a pair of sharp scissors to cut off the sleeves of your tee, cutting right at the hemline.

2. Then, cut the neckline. You can either just cut the hemline narrowly around the neck, or you can expand the neckline further by cutting more widely from shoulder to shoulder for a pretty boat-neck top.

Step 2

3. Cut the bottom hemline of your tee. But be careful when cutting this— depending on the original size of the shirt. If the shirt is extra large on you, you want to make sure to cut enough from the bottom so that the tee falls at your waist or hips. If the shirt is just right, you want to cut just above the hemline at the bottom of the tee. Also, remember, the edges will roll up slightly over the first few washes, so leave about a 1/2" extra length when cutting.

Step 3

3. It's a Cinch

This simple activity injects an instant shot of pizzazz to an otherwise hum-drum top.

Supplies:

- One of the following: Ribbon, silk or suede cord, a strip of netted fabric, or thick yarn—you'll need enough to go around your rib cage at least twice!
- Scissors
- Tank top or sleeveless tee
- Optional: Beads

Difficulty Level: Super Simple

What you do:

Step 1

Step 2

Step 3

1. Wind a cord twice around your mid-section and then cut it—this is your length of cord. Then, take your length of cord and cut it evenly in half.

2. Lay out your top flat in front of you. Then, take one of your lengths of cord and feed one end of it through one of the sleeves of your top, and have the end come out the head opening. Pull the cord so it is even between the sleeve and head opening.

3. Tie the ends of the cord together at the shoulder of your tank, so that the cord cinches all the fabric in between, and let the cord hang down your arm.

4. You can cut off the extra cord after you've knotted it, or just let it hang.

5. You can either do both sleeves, just one, or use different styles on each.

6. For an extra-funky touch, string beads onto the ends of your cord, putting a firm knot before and after each bead to keep them in place. (If the beads are still slidin', just double-knot!)

4. Star-Worthy Tee

Use crystals, rhinestones, or beads to make your tee shine.

Supplies:
- T-shirt with collar cut into a scoop-neck
- Pencil
- Fabric glue
- Any of the following—and as many as you want: Crystals, rhinestones, colorful beads

Difficulty Level: Super Simple

What you do:

1. Lay your tee out flat. Using your pencil, draw stars, hearts, or whatever shapes you like directly onto the tee.

2. Once you've finished your design, dot a bit of glue onto the back of a crystal, rhinestone, or bead.

3. Stick it onto the shirt, following your outline. Continue this process for your whole design.

4. If you'd rather create a more free-form design, glue jewels wherever you think they look best.

Awesome Accessories ★ ★ ★ ★ ★ ★ ★ ★ ★ ★ ★

Glam up your look with accessories you make yourself. The following projects are easy and fun! Some of them can make great gifts for BFFs!

Snazzy Shoes

Rhinestones, beads, and even adhesive patches can add oomph to so-so sneakers, flats, and flip-flops.

Supplies:

- A pair of shoes, either flats, sneakers, or flip-flops—depending on the design your choose
- Fabric glue
- Decorative embellishments, all of which can be found at a craft store: Assorted beads in different shapes, rhinestones, buttons, glitter, adhesive patches, fake flowers

Difficulty Level: Super Simple

What you do:

Like with Jazzy Jeans, how you decorate your shoes is up to you. Here are some fun ideas to try:

1. Use glue to adhere vintage buttons or flowers to the top of flats.

2. Glue rhinestones to the sides of your sneakers, along the trainer stripes.

3. Stick adhesive patches of various designs and sizes to the sides and top of slip-on canvas sneakers.

4. Glue rhinestones or beads to the straps of flip-flops.

Heady Headband

Use this recipe to create fun and funky hair décor.

Supplies:

- Bold scarf, fabric, or ribbon—the length should be long enough to wrap once completely around your head
- Plastic headband
- Scissors
- Fabric glue
- Optional: Beads and rhinestones

Difficulty Level: Super Simple

What you do:

1. Lay your piece of fabric out flat. Take your headband, and wrap the fabric around it. Then, trim the fabric into a strip that will fit length-wise around the headband.

Step 1

2. Apply a thin layer of glue to the top side of the entire headband. Center your strip of fabric along it, smoothing it down as you go.

3. Squeeze a layer of glue along the inside of the headband. Smooth fabric along the inside neatly.

Step 2

4. Trim off any remaining extra pieces of fabric.

5. Let the headband dry for at least 24 hours before wearing.

Style Secret: Twisty Ribbon Headband

Another funky and easy headband to make involves ribbon, scissors, and fabric glue. You'll want to cut a strip of ribbon at least three times the length of your headband. Then, apply a neat line of glue along the top side of the band. Next, beginning at an end, place the edge of the ribbon firmly into the glue and begin wrapping your ribbon around the band, overlapping slightly with each cycle. Pull the ribbon firmly, and smooth it down as you go. When you get to the other end, cut off any extra ribbon, and then add a little glue to the end of it and secure it to the headband. Let the band dry for 24 hours before wearing.

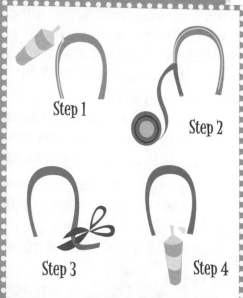

Step 1

Step 2

Step 3

Step 4

In the Bag

Spice up purses, backpacks, and gym bags with mini-mirrors, beads, and rhinestones.

Supplies:

- **Purse, backpack, or bag you're looking to spice up**
- **Fabric glue**
- **Decorative materials (use as much and as many different kinds as you prefer, based on your design and bag): Rhinestones, mini-mirrors, beads, adhesive patches, ribbon, fabric**

Difficulty Level: Super Simple

What you do:

First, choose a look—do you want a beaded-rose design or some lovely stripes? Next, plan out your pattern—you don't want to get midway through and find you've only got half the beads you need to complete the look you want. Then, lay out the beads on a table in the pattern you want. Do you have enough? How does it look? Mix it up until you're satisfied—then transfer the beads one-by-one onto your item, using fabric glue.

✳ If you're looking to bump-up the style on a backpack, just adding cool adhesive patches will do the trick.

✳ If you've got a blah black purse, dress it up by gluing rhinestones and beads on it in swirl, star, or heart-shaped patterns.

✳ For an Indian-inspired look, glue mirrors (found at bead, jewelry supply, and craft stores) in evenly spaced lines along your purse, or go random for a cosmo-look!

Beady Bracelet

Make a bracelet that matches your fave outfit, says your name, or spells out your fave band or brand...or get your beads into order with a sassy pattern!

Supplies:

- **Elastic thread**
- **Scissors**
- **Ruler**
- **Jewelry-making beads and/or alphabet beads. Depending on the size of the beads, make sure there will be enough to go around your wrist (do that by measuring the length around your wrist, then lining up the beads next to each other against a ruler).**

Difficulty Level: Super Simple

What you do:

1. Cut an 8-inch piece of elastic thread.
2. Tie a knot on one end of the thread.
3. String beads onto the elastic, creating your own unique pattern or words.

4. When the thread is full of beads, tie the two ends together so the bracelet fits snug around your wrist, and then cut off the extra thread. You can also separate certain beads by tying knots in the elastic.

Style Q & A

Q: My grandmother always buys me really ugly sweaters as gifts. Even worse, she always buys them two sizes up so they'll last a few extra years! They're not my style at all, but my Mom makes me wear them. Is there any way to make ugly sweaters look cool?

A: Sweaters definitely keep you warm and cuddly, but if they're not the right style for you, like any other clothes, they can look dorky! Luckily, there's tons of sweater camouflage that can make even the kookiest cardigan look almost...cool. First off, there's how you wear it. Stick on a turtleneck in the same shade and swing that puppy around your waist or shoulders. Or go layer-crazy: With a tee underneath, sweater on top, and unbuttoned blouse on top of that, people will be too distracted to pay attention to the big snowflake in the middle of your sweater. Still stuck? Well, if you can't beat 'em, join 'em! Find the most outrageous—but matching!—clothes you can, then try to make your hated garment look positively deliberate! You never know...you could start a new trend!

Q: How do you know how to match shoes to socks, and then to your outfit? My BFF always looks so cute, but my socks and shoes always look like they're just clashing with my outfits.

A: There's two ways to sure sock-success—matching them directly to your shoes, or matching them directly to your pants or skirt. Does that mean they have to be exactly the same color? Actually, no—but the shade should complement whatever you're planning to wear. So, hold those violet socks up to those red pants. Does it look kinda cool, or kinda strange? Place your blue slides next to them. How does it look? That's how it'll look when you put it on, too. Keep working until you've got a nice combo—or, just ask your BFF for some stylin' color help! After all, that's what's friends are for.

Q: I'm so psyched that spring's finally here! I'm happy about the change in weather, but I'm really stressed about my clothes, especially my shoes. It's too soon to break out my cutesy sandals and it's getting too hot to rock my fave clunky boots. What should I do?

A: With today's relaxed fashion, it's become easier than ever to step into spring! And it's all because of one word: MULES. Just think of the word as an acronym for Must UnLeash in Early Spring. Made with the weather and comfort of the season in mind, mules are the perfect, versatile, hip shoes to rock in spring. Put 'em on with your precious cargos, your diva dresses, or your classic denims! What's great about mules? They look good with all these styles.

Q: I grew a few inches in the last year, and my body's really changed. How do I know what will look good on me now?

A: Honestly, the best way is to hit the stores! Does that mean blowing all your allowance money in an hour? Of course not. But a trip to some favorite fitting rooms with a BFF can help you get a sense of what looks good on you now. So, look around at styles you've never tried before! If you've always worn knee-length straight skirts, try a long, flowy one. If you were stuck in straight-leg jeans, kick on some wide-leg jeans. Mix up different colors, cuts, and styles. Each time you find a piece you like, make a note. Then, when you're really ready to spring for a new collection, you'll have your signature style already mapped out!

5 RULES FOR THE ROAD

When crafting, ALWAYS...

1. Place newspaper, a drop cloth, or an old sheet down on your work area

2. Lay out all of your supplies before starting, so you know you have everything you need

3. Use "non-soluble" fabric glue, paint, or markers when designing clothes—that means it won't wash off!

4. Cap all glues and rinse all brushes when you're finished

5. Be sure to clean up!

Chapter 6

Awesome Accessories

Now that you've got your basic style-smarts down, it's time to blast your look to the next level. You don't need to have a ton of accessories to punch-up your wardrobe. Just a couple of things will add major kick. Some great basics are: A purse that goes with most of the outfits in your wardrobe, a nice necklace, a watch, a pair of earrings, a bracelet, a belt, a scarf, and a pair of sunglasses. Already got these covered? Great—it's time to add those amazing details that can make an only-okay outfit go from blah to blam! Just by adding on a bold scarf, a funky bag, dangling chandelier earrings, or a sparkly necklace, you can become a stylin' superstar.

You can also use accessories to completely transform your style—just swapping a plain leather belt for a studded one takes you from prep to funky, and a simple high pony with a flower-ribbon holder adds a flirty look to mere cargos and a tee. Think of it like decorating a cupcake—plain vanilla icing makes it look good, but dotting it with red-frosting hearts or pink and yellow flowers makes it irresistible!

But with so many accessory options to choose from, how can a girl keep them all straight—and, more important, from becoming a mess of mismatched mayhem? Don't worry—read on for the lowdown on jewelry, belts, hats, scarves, bags, sunglasses, and much more.

Bangin' Baubles ★ ★ ★ ★ ★ ★ ★ ★ ★ ★

One of the quickest ways to make your style more rockin' is to add jewelry. A bangle here, a sparkle there and *voilà*...instant glam.

Telling Time ★ ★ ★ ★ ★ ★ ★ ★ ★ ★ ★ ★

Besides keeping you from being late to class, a watch can do double-time as a bracelet. Because they come in a variety of shapes, sizes, colors, and styles, watches go with almost every outfit, occasion, and  style. There are endless possibilities—linked bands, metal, silver, gold, leather, and jewel-inset. Strips that are narrow, and bands that are wide. Bands with round, square, rectangular, and even triangular faces. Explore all the options, until you find one that speaks to you.

Earrings ★ ★ ★ ★ ★ ★ ★ ★ ★ ★ ★ ★

Want to stick out? Earrings are a girl's easiest everyday accessory.

* ✳ **Studs** are super-simple dots, the smallest earrings you can get. (If you get your ears pierced, the doctor will usually start you out with a pair of hypo-allergenic studs.) They usually come in pearl, diamond, silver, gold, or other gem or semi-precious stones. Don't be fooled—get nickel-free gold or stainless steel studs. These are the least reactive for those with sensitive skin.

* ✳ **Hoops** are round earrings in silver, gold, or stainless steel. Sometimes, hoops have embellishments like beads or diamonds, or ridging or patterning in the metal. Hoops can be so tiny they just barely loop around the earlobe—or so huge they practically graze your shoulders! (We don't recommend those for girls on the go.)

* **Dangle earrings** hang down from your ears. Sometimes, they're simply made up of one stone or bauble; sometimes they're a string of stones or a metallic coil. Dangle earrings are any kind that sway gently when you move your head from side to side.

* **Chandeliers** are big, sparkly danglers that look like (yep, you guessed it!) a chandelier. They're usually made of rhinestones or other semi-precious metals.

* **Clip-ons** are a great option for girls who don't want to pierce their ears. They come in all styles, and are usually sold alongside earrings for pierced ears. Be careful, though—an earring that's too heavy or clasped too tightly can cause irritation to your tender lobes, and you can have minor allergic reactions to the metal of the clip, even though it's only touching (instead of piercing) your skin.

Necklaces ★ ★ ★ ★ ★ ★ ★ ★ ★ ★

Get ready to stick your neck out...and throw your fashion style for a loop! Here are the major necklace effects.

* **Chains** are gold or silver links in various widths and lengths, and are often accompanied by hanging pendants or charms.

* **Pearls**, the jewelry-box staple of a classic look, come in strands of varying lengths. Their color can be white, gray, or even black, and their size can be pinpoint-tiny to the size of gumballs!

* **Rhinestones** are sparkly stones made of glass that come in tons of cool colors. Rhinestone necklaces vary in shape and style. Check out vintage stores especially for rhinestones—these necklaces were popular in the 1950s.

* **Chokers** are worn right up against the neck, often with an embellishment in the center. Chokers can be leather, beaded, or made of copper or steel. You can create a choker easily by placing a velvet ribbon flat against your throat and tying it neatly in the back, then letting your hair down to cover the tied bow.

* **Beads** make great necklaces and come in tons of colors, shapes, and sizes. Check out bead shops, if you'd like to string 'em yourself!

* **Cowrie necklaces** are made from cowrie shells, which have been pounded by the ocean. They're popular with surfers and skaters, and you can often spot guys and gals from warm-weather climates wearing 'em.

* **V-shape necklaces** hang in a permanent V-shape—they can be strung with stones or beads, or be totally plain.

Bracelets ✦ ✦ ✦ ✦ ✦ ✦ ✦ ✦ ✦ ✦

Don't be scared to take a *wrist*...bracelets are an easy way to arm yourself in mega-style!

* **Bangle bracelets** are big, oval hoops that slide over your hand, onto your wrist.

* **Cuffs** are wide bracelets with an opening in the back. Modern cuffs sometimes tie around your wrist.

* **ID bracelets** are often gold or silver links with a plate in the center for engraving a name or other word.

* **Charm bracelets** hold charms—little miniaturized objects that dangle. Some gals like to collect special charms to create a theme, like animal charms, shoe charms, travel charms, or musical charms!

Pins or Brooches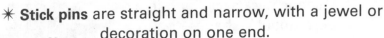

Sometimes a shirt needs an alert—give your *blah* tops pins and needles!

* **Scatter pins** are smallish, and can be worn together.

* **Bar pins** are horizontal bars with studs or jewels along the length.

* **Stick pins** are straight and narrow, with a jewel or decoration on one end.

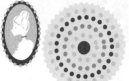

* **Brooches** (rhymes with COACHES) are large-sized, and come in many shapes and styles—a popular brooch is a **cameo**, which is an ivory engraving of a woman's face in a peach-shaped oval.

* **Button pins** are round and sport something on them—such as a design, a funny saying, or a political message.

Friends Forever

Sportin' Style: Fashion Tips for Wearing Jewelry

* If you want to sport a watch every day, go for one with a leather or metal band and a classic round face. This will match most of your clothes, last the longest, and can be used for all the occasions your singing Mickey Mouse timer can't.

* V-neck-shaped necklaces work best with tops that have unfussy necklines—try a boat or u-shaped collar. And definitely no turtlenecks, please!

* Don't pile your entire jewelry box on every day—go for one standout piece, and make everything else complement it. Go for signature looks with different fave outfits.

* Team a few (or more) bangles on your wrist. They look great with tank tops and with three-quarter sleeves.

* Rhinestones work great for dressy occasions, but stick to one or two pieces. For example, a pin and earrings work well, but if you've got them going on, skip the necklace. Or, if your necklace is really big, go for understated earrings. You want to be sparkly—not blinding.

* Chokers can make a long neck look shorter; a longer necklace can lengthen a neck; a necklace that rests in the space between your collarbones emphasizes the sweep of your shoulders. So highlight away!

Wrap Around ★ ★ ★ ★ ★ ★ ★ ★ ★ ★

Belts. Besides keeping your pants up, belts are like jewelry for your waist.

* **Chain Belts** are disco-mama-inspired silver- or gold-toned metal numbers that look like linked chains or loops. Some chain belts attach by a hook that allows some of the links to hang down.

* **Leather Belts** are, obviously, made of leather, with either a metal or leather buckle.

* **Western Belts** (*Yee-haw!*), AKA Cowboy Belts, are made of medium-to-wide leather and come with Texas-sized buckles.

* **Ribbon Belts** are sporty, thin canvas numbers that have either a flat metal buckle or loops that you thread the belt through.

* **Studded Belts** are made of wide black leather with silver metal studs.

* **Buckle Belts** have big, chunky funky buckles with elaborate details, like rhinestones, engravings, or fun shapes.

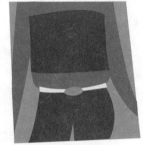

* **Seatbelt belts** are exactly what they sound like—belts made out of seatbelt material, with seatbelt clasps as fasteners!

Sportin' Style: Fashion Tips for Wearing Belts

* Don't wear a belt cinched too tight around your waist. Your clothes will pooch, making your stomach seem bigger and your clothes shlumpfy. Plus, it's uncomfy!

* If you're sporting a belt with a big, fancy buckle, be sure to tone down the rest of your jewelry. One large piece is enough—too much will overpower your outfit.

* Go for belts that are the same color—or that complement the colors—of your outfit. They help bring a look together. For instance, for a classic look, wear dark-colored belts with dark outfits, and brown belts with neutral-colored outfits. For a fun, springy look, try a red belt with a pink skirt, or a turquoise-y belt with olive khakis.

Scarves ★ ★ ★ ★ ★ ★ ★ ★ ★ ★ ★ ★ ★ ★ ★

Knotted around your neck, wrapped around your shoulders, or tied around your waist, scarves are one of the most versatile accessories. They come in three basic shapes:

Square   Rectangular   Triangular

Scarf Sense

Shapes are not the only thing to consider when wearing a scarf. There's tons of ways to knot 'em, tie 'em, and let them fly!

* Most scarves are made with a silky material and come in bright colors or bold patterns.

* Winter scarves are long, usually made of wool or cashmere, and often have fringes on the ends.

* Shawls are like scarves and can be worn either over your shoulders or around your waist. Shawls are usually triangular in shape and come in a variety of colors and fabrics. Pashmina shawls are wide, rectangular-shaped wraps worn around the shoulders.

Sportin' Style:
Fashion Tips for Wearing Scarves

✳ Tie a square scarf into a choker around your neck—but not too tight. You don't want to cut off your air supply!

✳ Loosely tie a rectangular scarf around your neck, with the knot hitting the collar of your top. Let the ends hang down.

✳ Let a square or triangle scarf hang knot-free—a great look with coats and blazers. Just make sure the scarf lays under your lapels for a clean look.

✳ Drape a triangular shawl or pashmina over your shoulders when wearing a dress, for a festive look. If the weather is warm, choose a light shawl and let it hang gently over the crooks of your arms.

✳ Tie a triangular scarf or shawl over a skirt like a wide, angled belt.

✳ Use a rectangular scarf as a belt, letting the ends hang down in the center or the back.

Sunglasses ✳ ★ ✳ ★ ✳ ★ ✳ ★ ✳ ★ ✳ ★ ✳

A must-have accessory, sunglasses protect your peepers from the sun, and they look cool, too. But picking the right pair can be tough, unless you know which style looks best on you. Let's start with frames:

Cat Eye

✳ **Cat Eye** glasses have oval frames that have pointy tips.

✳ **Coke Bottle** frames are round, like the bottom of a Coke bottle.

✳ **Square frames** are—*duh!* square-ish.

Coke Bottle

✳ **Aviators** were originally worn by pilots. These are flat along the top and rounded at the bottom, with dark or mirrored lenses and metallic frames.

Square

Aviators

* **Heart-shaped** frames are—*yep*—heart-shaped.

Heart-Shaped

* **Wrap frames** are often worn by action heroes or athletes during windy outside sports, like skiing. They wrap around the face.

Wrap

* **Large Ovals** have big oval frames that give wearers a glamorous, though bug-like, appearance.

Large Oval

The Right Frame for Your Face

Do you see what I see? Make sure your frames are the best match for your face-shape.

* **Round Face:** Go for square-shaped, oval, or cat-eye frames, which will all elongate your face.

* **Oval Face:** Lucky girl! Oval-faced girls can wear anything!

* **Long Face:** Oval and cat-eye shapes will make your face look more filled-out.

* **Heart-Shaped Face:** You look best with round and oval-shaped frames.

* **Square Face:** Large ovals will keep your face from seeming too angular.

The Shade of Your Shades

Sunglasses come in tons of colors, but the most popular frame colors are black, tortoise (a mottled brownish green), and silver or gold metal. But that's just the frame! The lenses come in almost as many colors as frames. The most popular colors are charcoal, green, brown, yellow, pink, purple, and blue.

The most important factor when buying sunglasses, however, is not the style or the shade but something else you have to check for on the tag: UV protection. "UV" stands for ultra-violet, which comes from the sun's rays, and can cause serious damage to your eyes if they're not blocked properly by UV protection on your lenses. So, while purple-mirrored shades may look fab, if they don't have UV protection, they won't protect your peepers from the sun or its glare…and you shouldn't use 'em!

Sportin' Style:
Fashion Tips for Wearing Sunglasses

✳ If you're a sporty gal, consider scratch-proof lenses with strong frames (not simple wires). You'll need this extra strength if you run around a lot and wear shades when performing in outdoor sports.

Rockin' Stockings ✳ ✳ ✳ ✳ ✳ ✳ ✳ ✳ ✳ ✳ ✳

Get a leg up on your legwear…and make sure you never *run* out.

✳ Pantyhose are made of nylon, silk, or lycra and go from toe to waist. Most come in a variety of neutrals—black, beige, white, pale pink—but you can find them in other colors, too. Fancy hose come with patterns, even rhinestones and other embellishments.

✳ Sheer hose are see-through. They come in all colors, and are a much thinner and lighter version of regular hose. They're best for formal outfits or evening wear, or in the warmer months, when you only need slight coverage.

✳ Tights are thicker than pantyhose and come in a variety of fabrics, such as cotton, wool, nylon, and lycra. They also come in tons of colors and patterns.

✳ Knee-hi socks or hose go up to your knees, and have a firm elastic band to keep them in place.

✳ Thigh-hi hose go to your thigh. They're held in place with a firm elastic band.

✳ Fishnet stockings are stretchy and look like diamond-shaped netting.

✳ Leg warmers look like long socks without feet, and were originally created for dancers to keep their legs warm while warming up. They became super-popular as a fashion statement in the 1980s, but were really thick and bulky. Current styles are much sleeker and softer.

Sportin' Style:
Fashion Tips for Wearing Leg Wear

✳ Tights, hose, and leg warmers come in dozens of patterns, from animal prints to hearts to flowers. Mix it up to go with different seasons, events, and looks!

✳ Matching shoes and hose give your legs a clean line, so go for black shoes when wearing black tights, navy tights with navy shoes, and so on, except with extremely bright-colored shoes. (Turquoise shoes and tights will overwhelm any outfit.) That's when you should stick to neutral colors.

✳ Opaque hose and tights work well for sportier looks and clunkier shoes. Don't mix opaque tights with evening wear, which calls for hose.

✳ If it's hot and you're wearing open-toed shoes, skip hose—just make sure your skin is well-moisturized.

✳ Pair thigh-hi tights in fun colors or patterns with boots and mini-skirts for a spunky look.

✳ If you're attending a formal event, buy TWO PAIRS of matching hose beforehand. Then, if your stockings rip while you're getting ready or—even worse!—during the event, you won't be stuck running around with a run.

✳ Care Tip: Tights and hose should be washed by hand with other delicate clothes, then allowed to drip-dry. Don't put any kind of hose in the dryer—it ruins the stretch and they'll run more easily.

Head Gear ★ ★ ★ ★ ★ ★ ★ ★ ★ ★ ★ ★ ★

Get on top of your look with a hat, scarf, or topper—and *head* them off at the pass! You can always decorate your 'do with the usual beauty accessories: Barrettes, headbands, ponytail holders, funky clips, decorative bobby pins, scarves, and, of course, hats. Here are the different options:

✳ **Berets** can be puffed up or pulled down at an angle on the head—major *ooo la-la*!

Beret

Skull cap

Baseball cap

* **Skull caps** keep the head warm in winter, but they also look majorly cool.

* **Baseball caps** are sporty alternatives for bad hair days, and great for keeping warm while exercising outside in cool weather.

Newsboy

* **Newsboy hats** are kind of like a beret with a brim—great for paper routes or bringing on fall fashions.

* **Panama hats** have a wide, khaki-colored brim and a string that can be tied around the neck. They're awesome for ripping through the jungle (*ha!*)—or just during a hot hike.

Panama

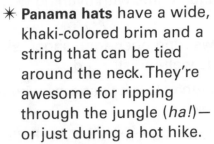

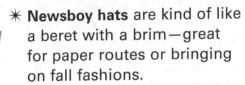

Sherpa

* **Sherpas** have fuzzy wool lining and flaps over the ears. *Brrr*—not anymore!

* **Cowboy hat**. Giddyup! Need we say more?

* **Sun visors** are basically a strap around your head with a brim to keep the sun out of your eyes.

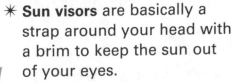

Cowboy hat

Sun visor

* **Wide brims** have—no surprise—wide brims, and were made fashionable by classic Hollywood movie stars.

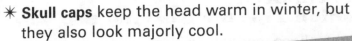

Wide brim

* **Fishing cap** is a basic round hat with a brim all around.

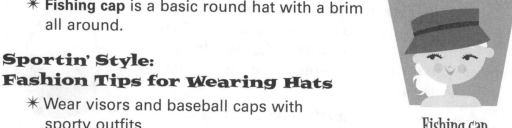

Fishing cap

Sportin' Style: Fashion Tips for Wearing Hats

* Wear visors and baseball caps with sporty outfits.

* Wear fishing caps with Capris and tees in the summer. It's a great hat to keep the sun from frying you as you go about your day!

* Wear wide-brimmed hats at the beach with your bathing suit and a pair of sunglasses for a touch of old Hollywood glam.

* Wear a newsboy cap with a blazer and jeans.

* Try a beret with a pencil skirt and sweater for a classic Outfit de Triomphe.

Bags/Purses ★ ★ ★ ★ ★ ★ ★ ★ ★ ★ ★ ★ ★

Even though it's oh-so-tempting to load it up with everything you love, your purse or backpack shouldn't double as a junk drawer! There's no need to lug around the entire contents of your room. Your bag should contain only the most important stuff you need during the day. Well, what are those? That's for you to decide, girl—can you not live without your amazing new gloss, that book you're lovin', or some dental floss?

Different occasions call for different types of bags—here's a rundown of the major kinds.

Clutch

* **Clutch:** A clutch is a strapless bag, usually shaped like an envelope. Because you've got to hold it in your hand, this is a better choice for a more formal affair than for a hands-on activity like shopping or going to school, which also require a bigger bag.

* **Handbag:** A handbag has handles and is carried by hand—you can't sling it over your shoulder.

Handbag

* **Shoulder Bag:** A shoulder bag, or purse, has long straps that go over your shoulder. These come in all kinds of sizes and styles, from mini-beaded for formal events to canvas catchalls for everyday wear.

Shoulder Bag

Backpack

* **Backpack:** A backpack can be worn over your back. These sturdy sacks are for the real heavies you need to lug around, like—*ugh!*—books and notebooks.

* **Messenger Bag:** These side-strap, soft-frame briefcases—based on the bags bicycle messengers use when they ride around the city—are a great alternative to backpacks. They've got a hip, classic look and they can give your outfit cool street credentials.

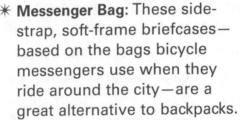

Messenger Bag

Tote

* **Tote:** A tote bag is somewhere between a backpack and a purse—it's almost as big and sturdy as a backpack, but it's got two straps you can sling over your shoulder. Totes are great for clunky stuff like beach towels 'n' slides, sleepover duds, or any other big items that you want easy access to.

* **Wristlet:** These teeny gems slip around your wrist and hold just enough for a night out. Perfect for movies with your buds or a dance—where you want your hands free to boogie down!

Wristlet

Sportin' Style: Fashion Tips for Carrying Bags and Purses

When figuring out what kind of bag is best with an outfit, you should think about how the bag works on YOU. In particular, you want to pay special attention to the bag's...

* **Shape.** Your bag's shape should be the opposite of your body. A structured bag works well with a fuller body, while a rounder bag works well with a lean bod.

* **Proportion.** Big bags on little girls look overwhelming. Very small bags on big girls look out of whack—go for a bag that's sized just right for YOU.

* **Color.** A bright bag makes a great splash of color on a neutral outfit—you don't want an acid-green coat to fight with a pink purse, unless you're really trying to make an eye-popping fashion statement.

* **Comfort.** You want to consider how comfortable your bag is, if it's something you're going to use every day. Does it bang against your hips? Do the straps dig into your shoulder? Take a walk around the store to try it out.

* **Roominess.** Can it hold all your stuff? Don't stick your schoolbooks into a purse—they'll drag so much you won't want to haul them to school and back. Not cool. If you've got homework—and we know you do!—you need a proper backpack. Don't like the standard styles? Hunt around for something that screams you.

* **Organization.** Will your purse keep you organized or turn into a junk drawer? Think about everything you need to carry with you and make sure there are enough pockets and compartments for your gadgets and stash-worthies.

Accessory Q & A

Q: What's up with scarves? Everyone at my school is wearing them!

A: Scarves are definitely in for the fall and winter seasons—but light scarves are fine all the way through spring! Scarves, which jazz up any outfit and can keep you totally warm, come in all kinds of fabrics, styles, and colors—from chunky wool ones that reach down to your feet to slim silk numbers that you can barely tie around your wrist. There's tons of interesting ways to wear scarves that are much less blah than the typical 'round your neck style. A few *GL* loves to sport are: Around your head (very French), tied around the handles of your bag, and around your waist as a belt.

Q: My school requires students to wear uniforms! I really don't want to wear them but we have to. Can you give me some tips to help make them fashionable?

A: Although uniforms may seem restricting, they allow you to be creative with your hair, nails, makeup, and accessories in ways that you probably wouldn't otherwise. Start with a funky hairstyle—experiment with braids, twists, knots, and curls. Tights and socks are also an awesome way to spice up your uniform—check out leg warmers, fishnets, patterned or polka dotted socks, and brightly colored opaque tights. Add sparkle to your uniform with jewelry: Try dangling earrings, silver hoops, a chunky bracelet, and lots of chain necklaces or pearls. You might also want to invest in funky scarves, bags, and shoes—these will give you a signature look even in same-as-her duds!

Q: My school doesn't let us wear hats in the classroom. What are some cool ones I can wear that are easy to get on and off and won't mess up my hair?

A: While it's true that hats are amazingly fashion-forward, tradition has it that they're still pretty disrespectful in class. And, while they're easy enough to take off, your average hat—of whatever style!—has a nasty habit of leaving a little ring-around-the-cranium. You can prevent nasty hat head by 1) sporting hats that are a little big (they'll leave less of a ring, and you can secure them easily with a bobby pin) and by 2) NEVER putting your hat on wet hair—your locks will dry in the exact shape of the hat's ring. There's also a tried-and-true hairstyle that always makes doffing your cap less traumatic: Pull your (DRY!) hair smoothly into a low pony or twist at the base of your neck before putting on your hat. When you take off the hat, run your fingertips over the crown of your head to smooth any stray hairs. Your hair should stay pretty—and ring-free!

5 RULES FOR THE ROAD

Here's some quick accessory know-how:

1. When choosing accessories, match the look to your clothing. Don't wear dangly earrings with sporty stuff—or sleek, modern jewelry or watches with frilly, girly outfits. Just check yourself in the mirror—do you blend or clash?

2. Don't overdo it! One or two accessories is enough for a look.

3. Arrange your accessories so they're easily found: Store all your bags and belts on neat hooks, and separate and organize your jewelry so that you can pick amongst faves easily.

4. Cheap bags, watches, belts, jewelry, and other accessories wear out pretty quickly. Save your dollars for the same style in a longer-lasting item.

5. Keep a file of pictures of jewelry, bags, watches, or other items you'd love to own. Then, when you get a windfall or have saved enough from babysitting or allowance, you'll know exactly what to splurge on.

Chapter 7

Shop So You Won't Drop

Now that you've passed Fashion 101 with flying colors, it's time to become a better shopper. Lesson numero uno: Getting great style doesn't mean you have to break the bank. With a little common sense and planning ahead, not only can shopping be fab pal-to-pal time, it can also be great for snagging major bargains. But before you hit the shops, read on to find out how to be a super shopper!

Shoppin' Savvy ★ ★ ★ ★ ★ ★ ★ ★ ★ ★

Follow these tips for a successful shopping spree.

* **Moola Management.** First, talk to your folks and determine how much you can spend. This will help once you're shopping because you can bypass items that don't fit into your budget.

* **Assess Your Assets.** Take a peek in your closet and see what you have. What's the basic color scheme? Which items do you continually not wear because you have nothing to wear them with?

* **What Do You Need?** Do you have the basics? If you don't, your best bets when shopping are to stock up on classic items.

* **Make a List.** Grab a notebook and jot down all the clothes you need. Then, list the things you want. Make a note of items you already own that need matching pieces. Keep this list with you while shopping. Try not to sway from it!

* **Dress Comfortably.** Shopping can be exhausting, so you want to make sure you're comfy. Wear clothes that you feel good in. Don't wear heels that are too high, since you'll be spending a lot of time walking and standing. (You can tote shoes with you to slip on when shopping, however.) Also, pass on clothes that are difficult to get in and out of.

* **Give Yourself a Shot of Confidence.** Shop when you feel good about yourself. Trying on clothes can be stressful. When you're feeling blue, clothes that don't fit can make you feel worse.

* **Know Before You Go.** Think about where you're going to shop and head straight to those stores. Having a plan will save time, especially if your time is limited.

Where to Shop ★ ★ ★ ★ ★ ★ ★ ★ ★ ★ ★ ★

If you want to get the best deals, the song had it right: You better shop around.

* *Department Stores* are the biggies—they're great places to shop because they have a lot of stuff. They also tend to be fairly reliable, with regular sales and flexible return policies.

* *Chain Stores* usually carry only one brand or few brands, and if you know what they have and if it fits you, it makes sense to continue to shop at them.

* *Specialty Stores* specialize in a particular kind or style of clothing, whether it's winter wear, all blue stuff, plus or petite sizes. Specialty stores are good for looking for something specific, like a cotton tee in a specific color or a particular kind of hiking boot.

* *Boutiques* are small stores that carry one-of-a-kind or designer items. They're usually pricey and don't have flexible return policies, but they can be a great place to splurge on a unique item or a one-of-a-kind accessory.

* *Outlets* usually offer clothes at a major discount. Outlet stores are a great place to stock up on trendy, one-season items or accessories. The problem with outlets is the quality of the clothing can be iffy and finding the perfect fit can be difficult.

* *Vintage* and *Thrift Stores* are great for finding deals on unique, vintage pieces, and even current styles. But, be sure to check for stains, rips, or tears before buying. Most thrift stores *don't* have a return policy.

* The *Internet* can be a reasonably priced and convenient way to shop. You can order most items from your fave department or chain stores online—or direct from your favorite designer. The one catch is that you can't try anything on. If ordering through a well-known store, it won't be a prob since their online return policies are usually the same as in-store policies.

cybershop

jeans

$49.95

buy now

Shopping ★ ★ ★ ★ ★ ★ ★ ★ ★ ★ ★ ★ ★ ★ ★ ★

A trip to the mall can be as easy as a walk in the park—well, almost.

Crowd Control. If you can, shop when the mall isn't crowded. There will be shorter lines for the dressing room and the cash register, and you'll have the salespeople to yourself. The best time to hit the stores is often during the week, right after school.

Time. Give yourself enough time. Don't try to find the perfect thing to go with your brown pencil skirt a half-hour before an event. Giving yourself plenty of time will make you feel less pressured, keeping you from impulse buying or from buying something you really won't like, or that doesn't end up fitting.

Shop for Yourself. Don't buy clothes that look good on your BFF or the store mannequin. You need to focus on what looks good on *you*!

Fit for Today. Go for clothes that fit your bod NOW—not the bod you want to have or think you'll have someday (or used to have).

Brand loyalty. Get to know the brands that fit you well, and go for those first when trying stuff on.

See It. Make sure you try everything on in front of a mirror, and, if possible, a three-way mirror, which will allow you to see the outfit from every angle.

Real Life. Buy clothes you'd actually wear—don't get yellow rubber boots just because they're trendy. Whatever it is, if you don't really like it, or if you don't like the way it looks on you, it'll just sit in your closet.

Sale Sucker. Don't get sucked in by sales. Just because something's cheap, doesn't mean you have to have it.

Multiplication. Buy things in multiples that fit you well—go for other colors or patterns that suit you. Having a variety of the same pieces will give you an ultra-comfortable wardrobe, and lots of options on those days you're running too late to spend an hour staring at the closet.

The Once-Over. Be sure to check out garments for quality. You should pay extra attention to details like buttons, seams, stitching, lining, zippers, and hems—it'd be a bummer to have your new skirt fall apart in the wash.

Hold It. If you're not quite sure about an item, have the store put it on hold, and think about it overnight or for a couple of days. This also works well for splurge items.

Mismatch. Does the piece match other things in your closet? If not, it's best to pass—you'll have to buy an entire new wardrobe to go with it.

Not Just for the Boys. Don't skip the boy's department. Boy clothes are often much cheaper than girl clothes—and more solidly made—and you can often find fab tees, sweatshirts, shorts, sweatpants, and even jeans.

Ask for Help. If you're unsure about an item, ask the salesperson for help. She should be able to help you find the right color and fit, or advise you against an item that doesn't quite work for you.

The Buddy System. Go shopping with a pal, sis, or Mom. They can offer honest opinions about clothes that do or don't work for you, help you get dressed, and find stuff for you when you're stuck in a dressing room with the wrong size.

Million-dollar Questions. Before you buy anything, ask yourself, "Do I *really* like it? Will I wear it a lot? Is it worth the price? Does it look good on me?" If you can't honestly say yes, it's best to pass— remember, you're saving your money for that must-have you'll see in another store!

Label It. Before heading to the cashier, read all labels to find out how you'll need to care for the item. If hand-washing or dry cleaning is difficult for you to deal with, you should probably pass unless it's a piece for a special event. A sweater that requires all kinds of special cleaning will spend more time in your laundry bag than on your back.

Sale Smarts ★ ★ ★ ★

Sales are ideal ways to invest in quality clothes you normally couldn't buy. Keep these things in mind when scoping sales.

* Find out when your fave stores have sales and try to shop then. Most salespeople will let a good customer know about upcoming sales in advance—so be polite and make friends!

* End-of-season sales can be used to stock up on winter items like coats, sweaters, jackets, and boots, and summer items like swimsuits, shorts, sandals, and sunglasses. That means shopping off-season, so get your flip-flops in September and your winter coat in April!

✳ When buying an item on sale, think twice—are you only buying the item because it's on sale, or because you really indeed like it? Be careful about buying a sale item you wouldn't purchase at full price.

✳ If an item you just bought goes on sale within two weeks after you bought it, take it back to the store and ask for the sale price to apply to your purchase.

Shopping Q & A

Q: I really like mini-skirts, but my mom hates them. How can I find a mini that my mom and I can agree on?

A: Where minis are concerned, there are two things to consider: How and where you're sportin' the shortenin'. To keep your mom happy, pair your mini with cute flats, and downplay looking too leggy. As for where, remember that your 'rents have the final say on appropriateness. When you can't agree, try the fingertip test: Standing with your arms held straight at your sides, the hems of your skirt should at least meet your fingertips. For school, don't go too much past just above the knee, if you can help it. (Leggy girls, we know it's hard!) A little compromise on both sides should keep mom mini-happy.

Q: Whenever I buy a new pair of shoes, I feel like I have to get a new outfit to match. Is that true?

A: The great fun—and danger!—of girls' shoes is that, unlike boys', they come in nearly every color, material, and style you can think of. If you buy a new pair of shoes to match every single outfit you have, that will leave your wallet empty (and you nearly buried in shoes!). A far better plan is to try to have shoes that match your major outfit categories instead. So, take a good look at your closet: What types of outfits do you usually wear? Are you a sporty girl? Then, go ahead and invest in a few pairs of sneaks—including one for hardcore exercising, and a few slip-ons to see you through other activities. Are you a girly girl? Try a few different pairs of kitten heels to cover your looks. Are you sleek and modern? One or two pairs of slip-ons or mules and a pair of boots should take you through. When you match your shoes to your overall looks, instead of owning a million pairs of different shoes that you can wear with only one thing, you'll have extra dollars to splurge for that ONE fab pair of lime-green sandals!

Q: I want to look cute for camp but still be able to move around. Help!

A: Camp is the ultimate test of clothes, where form definitely has to meet function. Here are two suggestions: Polo shirts and sport shorts. They're

comfy, and cute. Pair 'em with your sneaks, add a few stylin' hats and wristbands, and GO! You'll be ready to tackle any challenge, pose for any keepsake picture, and even look great when playin' cards on the floor of your bunk!

Q: My first school dance is coming up and I want to make a "big" impression. Any good tips for me?

A: Any dance is a time to look special, and you want a look that everyone will remember! Party dresses are a cool option that will give you a trendy, dressy look. To spark it up, go for something different. If you usually wear your hair up, wear it down (and vice versa). Usually rock plain studs? Go for some long, dangly earrings. If you've never tried a strappy sandal with a dress before, now would be a good time. Everyone will be talkin' about your new look!

5 RULES FOR THE ROAD

Don't buy things that:

1. **Don't fit**

2. **Don't match the rest of your clothes**

3. **Don't look good on you**

4. **Are in a color you'll never wear**

5. **Are so trendy, they'll be out before you leave the store**

Style Soundoff

Now that you know what looks good on you (and what doesn't!), and you've ditched the sweatpants, and have made a pact to give your outfits a little more thought, you're well on your way to being a style superstar. *What?* You haven't given up the grungy sweats?

You don't have to toss out your entire wardrobe, nor do you need to go out and buy a whole new one. Perfecting a look doesn't happen overnight. Attaining great style takes time and practice. And even then, there are days when you'd rather stay in your PJs than face the closet.

But hopefully, this book has given you some tools to stock in your fashion closet about what it takes to build a wardrobe and how to wear it well.

In the end, just know that superstar style is really achieved by feeling good about yourself: When you look good, you feel great. And when you feel good about yourself, your confidence will make any style stand out!